MY HEART TO HEART WITH LOVE

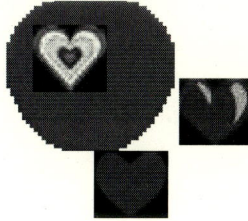

The heart is weary
Tired
Afraid
Amused
Captured
Feels pain

The heart is sometimes free
Lonely
Void of the troubles in the world

Ah the heart
The heart
The heart

It's unpredictable
Thus it loves again and again
Oh yes, there is true love
But for many, the heart loves; thus is feels the hurt and
pain of love over and over again.

Michelle Jean

It's really weird Lovey because this book is my heart to heart with you and I truly hope you comprehend and more than over stand what I am saying to you.

As humans are we not conditioned to believe in you?

Are you not thrown down our throats in the form of other deities?

Are you not whitewashed; the god of nastiness and perversion, and all that is evil?

Are you not the god of blood; keeping the bloodline of the selected few pure?

Are you not corrupt because you keep the nastiness of humans; man intact?

Are you not the founder and perverse leader that head the secret societies of man? Well not secret because people know about them and the nastiness that goes on in them; thus making you Satan of male and female origin that dominate and control this earth.

Are you not vile and nasty in the holy book and books of men because you indulge in incest; thus incest is predominant in man's so called holy book and here on earth? Therefore making you the father of incest and all that is perverse and nasty. You are perverse and nasty because man say you are and they say you are holy. So you cannot be clean, hence you are the filth and nastiness of this world; the cesspool of nastiness man follow here on earth. ***You Lovey is what's wrong with this world.*** *You are a condemnation because man; the males that wrote the so called holy book named the Holy Bible made you so.* **<u>SO IN ALL THAT MAN; MALES HAVE AND HAS DONE; THEY'VE MADE YOU THE FATHER OF NASTINESS AND YOU CANNOT REFUTE THIS BECAUSE IT IS WRITTEN IN THEIR HOLY BOOKS.</u>** *You have the Bible; man's so called holy book as proof. Thus I hold up my copy of this book for you to see and read.* **<u>This nasty and disgusting cesspool of garbage is what you let men and women including children preach from whilst they lie to humanity and say suck fuckry of nastiness is of you.</u>** *This garbage and fuck hole book of more than sin and blasphemy they say is divinely inspired. So yes you are to blame because you allow humanity to believe in all kinds of nastiness when it comes to you. Thus what say you come December, December 2015?*

You allow your children and people to hold their heads down in shame and disgrace to the shit MAN; HUMAN MALES WRITE ABOUT YOU.

<u>LOOK AT THE WAY THEY DEPICT YOU. AN INCEST PLAGUED BUFFOON THAT HAS NO MORALS OR</u>

CONSCIENCE WHEN IT COMES TO LIFE AND HUMAN DIGNITY.

You failed me, thus you failed your good and true people. No wonder many of us leave you because you are depicted as shameless; a god without shame and morals that is weak when it comes to the house and houses of sin.

Look at how Man; Males and Females mock life and the school of life.

Your pyramids are no longer sacred because the devil and their wicked and evil people infiltrated your own kingdom and brought you Lovey to your knees.

How shameless and disgraceful are you?

You let shit happen then you want us to look to you.

How can anyone look to you for the truth when you allow men; disgusting filth of nastiness to represent you? Men; males are the vile and corrupt ones but yet you give them a home here on earth.

You allow them to control, dominate and kill and there isn't a damned thing you can do about it. Well no there is, there's hell and shortly hell will be unleashed on billions here on earth so I truly take that back though I doubt myself and you on this day.

Nasty are you, thus man; humans bask in the nastiness and nasty communities and communal settings and societies of man.

Blood is nasty thus many drink blood and bask in the nastiness of inbreeding. Thus many of our ancestors; your good and true people gave up true life long before their so called Adam and Eve to join the bloodsuckers of hell until this day. Thus Satan loves black people and the inbreeding will never stop. Meaning blacks marrying the devil's true and lowly own. *So now tell me Lovey, if we are born from the same seed; nastiness in life, what the hell does that make you?*

Doesn't that make you nasty too?

According to the filthy shit box of garbage that man is given to read and profess as holy, did not Eve come from Adam her father as made by you? And did not father turn around and sleep with daughter and have kids with her? So tell me Lovey, if you did this, are you not cut from the same nasty and filthy life and gene; cloth?

Are you not a nasty gene and spirit thus GENESIS; THE GENES IS? Wow because I am going ballistic on you. You made man depict you as a monster in their nasty book; a book that keeps humanity nasty.

A book that they say is from you.

YES I KNOW THIS BOOK IS TRULY NOT FROM YOU LOVEY BUT I HAD TO GO THERE TO SHOW YOU JUST HOW NASTY AND FILTHY YOU ARE IN THE EYES OF MAN; HUMANS; THEIR BOOK.

Man write lies about you and you bask in it.

Man say this book of condemnation and corruption is holy and billions believe in it; swear by it. But what do you say Lovey?

What are you truly going to do come December, December 2015?

Yes I am tired and I am tired of the lies that's circulating out there when it comes to you.

Yes Zion fell but what say you Lovey?
Truly what say you?

Yes this book is negative but I have to come to you in this way because you are truly not fair, nor are you just and true to yourself.

Think and do better for self.

The lying bullshit of you must stop. You cannot continue to let the devil's people take your glory and people from you.

You cannot continue to allow humans to think you nasty; filthy, corrupt and condemned come on now. I truly love you but you need to truly love yourself.

NO HUMAN BEING OR SPIRIT ON THE FACE OF THIS PLANET AND BEYOND SHOULD BE SUBJECTED TO THIS TYPE OF FILTH AND GARBAGE AS WRITTEN IN THE BOOK AND BOOKS OF MAN; MAN'S SO CALLED HOLY BIBLE. MORE IMPORTANTLY, YOU SHOULD NOT BE SUBJECTED TO THIS TYPE OF GARBAGE AND LIES COME ON NOW. THIS IS YOU LOVEY. WHAT GIVES HUMANS THE RIGHT TO DEFACE YOU LIKE THIS? YOU GAVE US LIFE AND WE DU YU SOH!!! THE FILTH THAT MAN; HUMAN MALES WRITE ABOUT YOU TO KEEP THEIR NASTINESS AND NASTY SOCIETIES GOING IS WRONG BUT YET YOU HAVE NOT VINDICATED YOURSELF WHEN IT COMES TO THESE LIES.

I know there is hell, but who the hell can wait when it comes to shit written in man's Holy Bible and other books about you. Yes I know I get angry at you and go ballistic on you, but I truly need you to care about you. You gave us good life and you gave us Will; the right to choose between good and evil and man did choose the latter over you, I get it. But tell me why the lies against you to send and or plunge all of humanity into hell with them?

The corrupted condemnation of worse than cesspool and stench say they are Jews Lovey. They say they are your people but YET PUT YOU IN THE NASTY BRACKET OF SATAN AND HIS BABYLONIAN FILTH.

Man's so called holy bible is not of you Lovey and you know this. *So why let the devil's people use your true people; the true Jews and your name like this?*

WHY ALLOW THIS MASSIVE CONDEMNATION OF HUMANITY LOVEY?

WHY TAKE YOUR GOOD AND TRUE PEOPLE FROM YOU?

WHY LET EVIL TELL LIES ON THEM AND YOU LIKE THIS?

I truly love you and have been subjected to this nastiness, but I found the truth in you even though I come to you in this way. I have to bring my doubts, my truths, my happiness and anger to you. Lovey you have to be true to you, so stop letting the devil's people use you like this. They are not one of us, so truly keep them at bay forever.

• • •

Lovey, December is approaching and I need you to be vindicated of all the lies Man and all of humanity tell on you. Lovey you are not disgusting and filthy but yet men; humans depict you as disgusting and filthy.

Lovey, you have man's lying book of the lies they tell on you so vindicate yourself. You have to.

These vile and disgusting condemnations of sin need to be more than infinitely and indefinitely locked in hell more than forever ever without end with no chance of parole and escape. They sell lies against you Lovey and you give them the glory why?

Why do you condemn yourself with man?
Why do you hate yourself so?

Are you suffering from depression Lovey?
Do you not see the true beauty in you?
Do you not care about you?
If you do, then truly love you come on now.

Yes it's a different me today hence my harsh words and my heart to heart with you. You know me Lovey, so truly love you and yes truly love me and not love me so.

Why should man and or humans lie on you so?
Take it all from them and let them see their own hell; end Lovey come on now. Condemn them all for the lies they spread against you and preach about you. ***You do not tell***

lies on humans; so why are humans telling lies on you and falsifying you?

Tell me, are you my true father? A true father would not sit down and let people who are truly not his people tell lies on him. Yes I know you are truly patient and it's not the big things that get to you but a lie is a lie Lovey. *Yes, I KNOW THERE IS NO EVERLASTING LIFE FOR THEM BUT ETERNAL AND SEVERE PAIN AND SUFFERING IN HELL LONG AFTER ALL OTHER HUMANS HAVE EXPIRED.* I know this Lovey, but I cannot bare to see these vile cesspools of wickedness preaching and teaching lies against you. *I CANNOT STAND TO SEE THEM PUTTING YOU AND YOUR NAME IN THEIR NASTY BRACKET OF DUNG.*

Maybe it's me Lovey and I overly truly more than truly and unconditionally truly love you, but it cannot be helped. I am in a different frame of mind and if I could lock these demons of worse than hell and dung away right now and let their empires and bank account crumble to zero; I would. *Yes I know this is my sin when it comes to you but what gives anyone the right to take good and true life from you?* And please truly don't go there with WILL thus the ugliness of some of our spirits. I know and get it but Lovey, but for me; truly vindicate you and yes me come December, December 2015. I need to see the devil's empires crumble globally with no chance of ever rising again. I need earth to truly replenish herself and live in true peace without the evils of man; humans. I need our good and true environment to be safe Lovey because I do want and need to see you face to face. I truly need what's best for you and evil is truly not best for you and you know this.

Truly consider you Lovey because you are truly worth it. No man, woman or child including spirit and beast should falsify you and tell lies about you. I will not permit this any longer so truly love you. And despite me saying life isn't worth it sometimes. I KNOW GOOD AND TRUE LIFE IS TRULY WORTH IT.

It is truly hurtful and painful for me Lovey and you truly know this. How can a man or anyone look to you and say you are this nasty and filthy?

How can anyone write books of nastiness and say they are of you; from you and or divinely inspired?

You told me to write a book and all you've given me is the truth. I know she said, God kills but Lovey, did you not send the white men in blue to tell me to "WALK BEFORE DEATH?" Have I not been trying to walk before death?

Did she not thank me for outing them one by one?
Have you not given humans time to amend our dirty ways and we are the ones to refuse to clean up ourselves?

Did you not show me the different sins of humans in terms of what their spirit look like? So Lovey, how can you let humans depict you like that in their books; so called holy books? It hurts man come on now. It hurts and the tears are there.

You created it all and humans kill it all for what?
What respect do we show you?

Billions worship other gods and idols and say they are you and you're okay with this; well I'm not. I cannot be okay with this because you are not man; human. You are not fleshy even though I've compared you to a fleshy to get my point across. But Lovey, do better for you by having some ambition for self. I can't preach to you anymore. You cannot continue to hold on to hope when it comes to our black own because our black own do not care about self, nor do they have any self respect. See how I've tried to help my own and look at the disrespect I got.

My grandmother is a perfect example of how she tried to help others and look at the disrespect she got.

More importantly, YOU ARE THE TRUEST EXAMPLE OF HELP AND HOW YOU TRY TO HELP HUMANITY AND LOOK HOW HUMANITY TREAT YOU. THEY DEPICT YOU WORSE DAN A DEMON OF HELL WHEN IT COMES TO FILTH AND NASTINESS. WI DISRESPEK YU AN SPIT PAN YU. WI TRAMPLE YU DUNG AND KILL YU. So tell me, why do you continue to try with people that spit on you and trample you down daily? Lovey I truly can't take anymore man come on now. I should not have to show you this because you see it already.

I should not have to talk to you this way because this is not your true way of life nor is it mine.

I should not have to cuss you out nor should I have to hold my head down in shame and disgrace to the way humans depict you and treat you.

So tell me, how can I continue with you when humans truly do not hold you in high regard?

How can I hold my head up and say I am truly proud of you, when you of yourself is not truly proud of you to the way you let humans depict and disrespect you?

You are not a caged animal, so truly do better for you because no human being has or have the right to do this to you. We have and has lost our place and respect; thus you cannot give us a home with you because we truly do not respect and count you. Wi count yu out; thus yu a count out fi many in society globally come on now.

Truly think and do for you because **HUMANS ARE TRULY NOT DOING FOR YOU. THEY ARE DOING FOR DEATH HENCE THEY PAY DEATH AND KEEP DEATH ALIVE.**

You are the greatest; now truly vindicate you as of December, December 2015 and beyond. Bring these lying cesspools of sin and condemnation called men, holy men and women including children that walk in the way of evil and lie about to their knees indefinitely more than forever ever without end. They are demons that sell the Satanic Agenda. They have nothing to do with truth or you Lovey because they condemn you and embarrass you with their lies and deceit. Absolutely no one that is truthful to you can lie on you or lie about you come on now. Even I know this. Hell is their domain because they sell death; hell, thus hell must now begin to take them. Death is their god thus death must now walk and take them to hell along with their congregation. Death can no longer plague your good and true people Lovey; thus death must show their faces to those lying bastards that deceive humanity when it comes to you. All the monies they rob society and people must go with them to hell; thus their sentence in hell must include the money and monies they stole; rob from humanity and this earth.

Further, because they brought condemnation to earth with their willful and blatant lies of you Lovey, earth must retreat; take away her blessing from them and the land they live in. Earth must vindicate her as well because the lies of these men and women including children as well as others; did cause you to flee from her also (earth). Earth can no longer yield her goodness to many of these lands because ***MEN; HUMANS DID SET UP WHORE HOUSES IN THEIR LAND AND LANDS FOR DEATH. THUS***

CONDEMNING THAT LAND AND PEOPLE UNIVERSALLY, GLOBALLY AND SPIRITUALLY.

Spiritually billions are condemned thus death must purge earth of their wicked and evil people and spirits. This must begin to happen as of December 2015 Lovey because December and every December from henceforth truly belong to us. Evil can no longer store up evil anywhere in earth, on earth, in the universe or in the spiritual realm. All evil must begin to vanish thus December 2015 is vital to the existence of truth and all that is truthful Lovey. You have your day and we have our day together. So truly, truly, truly love you in truth because ***no matter how mad I get at you, and no matter how harsh I am with you, and no matter how disrespectful I may seem to people, you are my true worth and you are truly worth it to me.***

I need you to wake up and do for you and your good and true people. I need all sin and evil to be gone from this earth so that we can enjoy life here on this earth with you.

Let the end come for all who are wicked and evil because death was their choice and not you. Come on now man truly do and truly love you.

I can't quarrel with you anymore for your own true good. Man; human males wrote books of lies against you. Stop being patient with man now man come on now. Do something to correct the damage. Man wrote lies about you and for centuries you've kept this lie going. The lies have to stop. She told me God kills and I defended you. Defend you now come on now. I know death is a god but stop letting Death screw good and true life; you.

Stop letting death's children and people make this earth their stomping ground and yard for their cesspools of sin and wickedness; sacrifices unto other god and gods.

I truly love you and I truly need what's best and right for you, so truly think and help me to truly help you. I can't cry anymore for you now man come on now. I can't do it all by myself. You shouldn't have to live this way. We as humans should not have to believe in lies when it comes to you.

The truth of you NEED TO BEGIN AS OF DECEMBER, DECEMBER 2015 AND ALL THE DEVIL'S KINGDOMS HERE ON EARTH MUST BEGIN TO PAY FOR THE LIES THEY SPREAD AND TELL ABOUT YOU.

I need this for you Lovey, so truly help me to make your home and world including mine truly clean and whole again so that we can be truly free to live in goodness and in truth; total cleanliness. We need to be happy and lies do not make anyone happy in the long run. Lies bring pain, shame and disgrace, and humanity has shamed and disgraced you long enough. You are Lovey, the creator of ALL hence Allelujah and Allah for some. Both good and evil cry out to you, but you have to start ignoring evil and start accepting and listening to the good and true people of this earth. Those that truly and unconditionally truly love you and think of you in all that they do. You are almighty; meaning you are our truth, so truly stay truthful to us and let evil go. You cannot accommodate evil anymore nor can earth and this universe including the spiritual realm accommodate them. ***Hell was the choice of billions so give them the hell that they choose.*** I am tired of humans disgracing you and putting death over life come on now. You Lovey are our good and true life, so let go of death because death is death and death is truly not worth it. Life is more than worth it hence you are the choice of the selected few and you know this. You cannot hold on to death Lovey, you have to hold on to true and good life. You are clean hence clean must separate and segregate themselves from all that is dirty come on now.

It's like different nations have their depiction of you, but are you not a he she? Male in the spiritual realm and female in the physical realm?

Are you not confusing to humanity and instead of breaking down the walls of confusion and pain including shame; you let this confusion continue even in me? So how can we know you and ask you for help if along the way we've truly lost you and forgotten what you look like?

Yesterday (October 17th 2015 was a different day for me thus I wrote what I wrote and I will not take my writings back. I have to move forward in a positive way.

Let me ask you something Lovey. Why do you ask for something when you of yourself know that it cannot be given unto you?

Why do you pretend to care when you truly do not care?

I mean, no I do not mean. Hence I am going to ask you this and please truly do not feel a way because this is me from yesterday to today. I am not insulting you but from the way things are going in my life and given the observation of you, ***ARE YOU A DOG?***

Do you not treat us like puppy dogs?

Do you not leave us to fend for ourselves?
So are you a dog?

Are we not conditioned to think you are this more than powerful being that can do it all when you truly cannot?

Are we not living by your false hope and the false teaching of man globally?

Do we not worship and praise Amon-Ra the Egyptian God instead of you?

Do we not pray to him and close with him when we say Amen?

Do we as humans not praise and worship men as our god and gods?

Yes some worship and praise females also but truly, who are you Lovey? Who are you truly when it comes to the physical and spiritual realm?

Now tell me who have I been giving my true love to all this time because praise and worship it seems dates back to Egypt?

Why is that Lovey? Is it because Egypt was conquered by the Babylonians after Ethiopia?

Is it because the evil and lying and yes defiling Babylonians changed our books of truth to include them and their nastiness of paganism and death; sin?

Why keep us in the dark when it comes to the truth Lovey?

So are you truly a dog?

ARE YOU ANUBIS?

Now tell me Lovey, why do we praise and worship Egyptian deities when originally Egypt had no deities?

Did not the Babylonians introduce their false idols and gods to Egyptian culture and Moses had to take life; the truth out of Egypt and bring it to a foreign land? Well not a foreign land but a land where black people lived. Thus China has the Ying and Yang until this day. Moses had to take the truth out of Egypt because if the truth stayed there it would have been fully corrupted. Also, did not the book of death tell you of the struggles Moses had with his people. When he went up into the mount and came back he saw his people worshipping a golden calf. We know idols are not of you thus Egypt became the stomping ground of death and sexual perversion of every kind.

These idols can't do anything but yet we are conditioned to praise and worship them whist thinking they are you.

NOW TELL ME THIS LOVEY. WHY ARE WE CLOSED OFF FROM YOU AND WHY CAN'T WE CONNECT TO YOU HERE ON EARTH?

See when I talk and or reach out to you like this, it does something to my spirit. It's as if my spirit want to leave my body but can't because of the prison walls of my cranium. Now my head is beginning to hurt because my spirit is trapped inside my body; head and truly cannot leave at will. What a pity.

It's such a shame Lovey that we've been conditioned to accept Egyptian deities that was based off Babylonian god and gods.

It's a shame that we in humanity cannot see this, thus the control and hold Babylonian deities have on civilization and modern day civilization until this day.

So in all I seek, I see and know the truth of you including the lies of you and it is truly a shame.

So what is the purpose of life Lovey when life is falsified has no true merit when it comes to you and the truth?

What good are you to humanity when there is no trust in you due to the lies we've been told and still being told?

These lies are centuries and generations old Lovey but yet throughout the course of history, you let these lies stay and have not done anything of substance to debunk them. So if you cannot debunk the lies that surround you and being told on you, how can we as humans expect you to truly save us? *How can we accept you as God and Father?* Lovey we are being fed lies about you thus all we know are lies. So if we know lies; the lies of you, are we not going to continue living in these lies? Are we not going to tell lies and continue sinning each and every day?

• • •

Are we not going to constantly fail you?

Now tell me this, what right did man have to take the records of Egypt and falsify you; them?

Why break the black civilization and bring them to their knees Lovey?

Why let wicked and evil people destroy you and your people? So with all this said, you were not strong enough. Now I ask you, when did you get weak?

When did evil defeat you? No don't answer that because I know our people let evil into our realm and nothing that you have and has done can get rid of evil. Dem cum eene like ticks to yass. Not even jayze can get rid a demya ticks ya to claate. So yes I know the truth.

So Lovey, why are you so weak still?

Why do you still want to be associated with the Egyptian lies that are being told and spread about you?

Now tell me this Lovey, why should I stay with you knowing all of this?

I want nothing to do with Egyptian deities and falsities. I need my true living and truthful Lovey; father that truly protects and surround our people so that no manner of evil and wickedness can come near us or infiltrate us.

What is the purpose of calling out to you Lovey when you cannot do this or take us out of the countries and households of the wicked and evil? Why keep us amongst the corrupt and sinful of this world?

I've asked you in some of my other books which are our books, if we are told and given lies, are we not going to come an accept these lies? Will we not become liars also?

So if father is a lie his children will become a lie also. You know this because ***lies cannot beget truth, they can only beget lies.***

A negative cannot become a positive; it is still negative because the original source is negative. ***No matter HOW YOU PUT A NEGATIVE AGAINST OR AMONGST A POSITIVE YOU WILL NEVER GET A POSITIVE YOU WILL GET A NEGATIVE.***

Negative forces dirty and kill. *SO TRUTH WILL ALWAYS BE KILLED BY THE WICKED AND EVIL AND YOU CANNOT CONTINUE TO LET THIS HAPPEN.* The time of death is over and now it's time to clean house of all its evil indefinitely without end more than forever ever. Sin and evil have to go come on now. Who want to continue to live in stench? I certainly don't come on now.

Earth and your good and true people cannot take the blow and blows of sin and death anymore. You have to truly help us Lovey. We cannot fight for you and the goodness of you and you're not helping. You can no longer be like the weak. You have to be strong because truth can overcome all that is evil come on now. You are our strength, so get up and stand with us in truth. Truth cannot fail no matter how evil do all to kill the truth. Evil dies but truth cannot die come on now. You know this.

You asked me to do something but yet where are the tools; the right tools to acquire your home.

Go back to Real Situation by Bob Marley Lovey and truly think. Humans; more specifically men are positioning themselves to rule under one world order shortly. These men seek global domination and no one can stop them from another angle. Humans globally gave these men power to invoke and enchant the dead. They made their sacrifices unto the dead and not even you Lovey can stop them from taking rulership of this earth. These men dictate what goes on globally because they have the clergy to back them. They have Lawyers, Doctors, Politicians and yes People of Society to back them. You know this and yes I shouldn't say this because I know hell will be unleashed on earth real soon and many are going to lose it all shortly.

These men also have the clergy to write books of lies about you so that they can control and deceive; keep humanity from saving self in the end.

But in the end the clergy cannot save them because the CLERGIES OF THE WORLD HAVE AND HAS BEEN CONDEMNED BY YOU LITERALLY. There is absolutely no hope for them because they did lie about you and caused all in humanity to turn against you literally. So yes I know the truth and full truth of you despite me saying otherwise.

So yes I know the truth but despite that, I am going to continue on in my doubtful and yes sinful manner. I need you to see and know Lovey. I need a positive change in you and if doubting you is the way to send you this message then so be it. ***I do not regret doing this, speaking to you in this way because this is my heart to heart with you. I have to let you know how I truly feel. It's not all about humans Lovey, it's about you also. It's about cleanliness and this world; earth and or environment. Truth must prevail at all cost come on now. Let evil go and let us truly live come on now.***

In all you did Lovey, you permitted this happen. So as Bob said and on another level, "ain't no use, no one can stop them now," and he's truly correct. ***YOU LOVEY IS BANNED FROM EARTH BECAUSE MEN MADE SURE THE EARTH WAS DIRTY FROM THEIR SINS.*** Man played you thus the lie is recognized and believed by humans globally until this day.

Humans gave the enemy; evil victory over you Lovey because it's the book of evil humans preaches and teaches from.

It's the book of evil that captures their soul and or spirit (the souls of humans and spirit) and brings it to hell with them. Thus the body and spirit has and have become sacrifices unto death by others. And it's as if humans can't see this nor do they want to know this.

It's this book of evil that depicts you Lovey as a succubus that drinks blood and or deal in blood, incest and blood sacrifices.

This book, man's so called holy bible is man's book.

MAN'S HOLY BIBLE AND OR SO CALLED HOLY BOOK IS THE ELITE'S AND OR THE NASTY BOOK OF ROYALS THAT DEPICT THEIR NASTINESS AND CONDEMNATION.

THIS BOOK CAN NEVER BE YOUR BOOK LOVEY, NOR CAN IT BE DIVINELY INSPIRED BY YOU.

IT IS THE BOOK OF DEATH THUS HUMANS FOLLOW THE LIES AND BELIEVE IN THE LIES OF THIS BOOK WITHOUT KNOWING THAT THEY ARE GOING TO DIE.

THEY ARE ALL HELL BOUND BECAUSE THEY BELIEVE AND TRUST IN THE NASTINESS AND LIES OF THIS BOOK.

FURTHER, THEY BELIEVE THAT THIS NASTY BOOK OF CONDEMNATION AND SIN IS OF YOU LOVEY. SO IF THEY BELIEVE THIS FILTHY BOOK CALLED THE HOLY BIBLE IS OF YOU, _HOW CAN YOU SAVE THEM?_

ARE HUMANS NOT SAYING YOU ARE AS NASTY AS MAN; THEM?

So truly what say you Lovey come on now? Talk to me because this is not just my heart to heart with you but your heart to heart with me. Truth needs you, so truly look to truth because you have it in your chosen few come on now. ***YOU HAVE TO FULLY WALK AWAY FROM HUMANITY AND THEIR NASTINESS. YOU CANNOT SAVE WICKED AND EVIL PEOPLE THAT PUT YOU***

ON THE SAME LEVEL OF NASTINESS WITH THEM.
YOU ARE CLEAN NOT DIRTY AND HUMANS FAIL
TO REALIZE AND RECOGNIZE THIS.

Not because we have WILL does it mean we are to live unclean and wallow in the filth of nastiness like pigs.

We as humans live like hogs because we fight against each other, we hate each other and we kill each other. So why should you Lovey save hogs that live like pigs?

Pigs are not clean; they are nasty; not just in the physical realm but in the spiritual realm also. Demons are nasty well some of them, but pigs are nastier and you Lovey know this.

HUMANS FAIL TO KNOW, RECOGNIZE AND SEE
THAT THEIR SO CALLED HOLY BIBLE WAS GIVEN
TO THEM TO PLUNGE THEM INTO HELL BY THE
ROYALS AND NONE CAN SAY OTHERWISE
BECAUSE IT WAS A ROYAL; KING JAMES; A NASTY
MAN THAT COMMISSIONED THIS NASTY BOOK
TO BE WRITTEN. NO ONE IN HUMANITY CAN SAY
OTHER WISE BECAUSE NASTY MEN AND WOMEN
INCLUDING CHILDREN READ, PREACH AND TEACH
FROM THIS NASTY BOOK DAILY. Yes I know the books of Egypt Lovey thus I tell humanity, Psalms One is

the truest Psalms in man's nasty book. Thus good and evil cry out Allelujah and those other demons say Allah. They want to get in but none can get in with the exception of those that converted to this religion without knowing the full truth. They have a saving grace and will forever have a saving grace. I will not change this, but as for Babylon and or Babylonians; they will never get a saving grace from you or me Lovey. ***They are truly condemned thus they are the true and unconditional WHITE RACE; DEATH.*** *And no matter how they say they are one of us, and are willing to convert and or change;* ***absolutely no saving grace is given to them. I REFUSE TO ALLOW IT; THUS DECEMBER FOR REAL.*** You have your day Lovey and you can forgive them if you want or so desire, but I will never forgive them for taking us from you. You do not take a person's right from them and bring them to hell with you come on now. ***IF YOU AS A RACE AND NATION WERE TRUE; LOVEY'S LIFELINE WOULD HAVE EXTENDED TO YOU.*** But because you have no good will for humanity and you lie and deceive nations; call them slaves, steal their heritage and culture; pollute the realms of earth and this universe with your idol and animal worship; you will never get a way it. ***Lovey is forbidden to look upon you too and yes this is from my perspective and point of view.***

Yu tink mi done!! Not even in life or death will I consider any of you to what you have done to Lovey and his people.

• • •

Please, find Lovey on your own if you can because no entry is given to any of you.

True Jews must not associate with Babylon and their people. Therefore none of us can marry any of you. YOU ARE TRULY NOT ONE OF US. YOUR GOD IS YOUR GOD AND GODS; IDOLS. YOU PRAISE AND WORSHIP DEATH _THUS YOU KILL LIFE ALL AROUND AND MOCK THE BREATH OF LIFE. Every true Jew globally is forbidden from marrying you and Jews; the true Jews know this. We; the true Jews have the key to stop the nonsense that is happening here on earth including in the universe, and shortly it is going to stop because death cometh for their own before 2032 on a massive scale._

THEREFORE, I AM TRULY GLAD NO ONE CAN CONVERT TO LIFE; YOU HAVE TO LIVE LIFE GOOD AND TRUE; HONEST AND CLEAN. ABSOLUTELY NO ONE CAN CONVERT TO LIFE LOVEY AND YOU KNOW THIS. SO TRULY GOOD LUCK TO THOSE WHO HAVE CHANGED THEIR GOOD UP GOOD UP SELF AND LIFE FOR DEATH. Soon you will see the hell you face because you made it so for you and your family; children if you have them.

HUMANS ARE THE ONES TO CHOOSE EVIL WILL.

SO WHAT WE AS HUMANS CHOOSE AND CHOSE WITH THE EXCEPTION OF THOSE WHO ARE GIVEN A SAVING GRACE YOU MUST DIE; HAVE TO DIE BECAUSE EVIL AND OR DEATH WAS THEIR CHOICE IN THE LIVING.

ANYONE THAT HAS CHOSEN DEATH WILLINGLY AND WILFULLY IN THE LIVING CANNOT BE SAVED. DEATH IS YOUR CHOICE AND YOUR CHOICE IS ON RECORD SAYING YOU CHOSE DEATH IN THE LIVING AND NOT LIFE.

We've forgotten that once you choose and or chose death here in the living; you must go to hell and die; burn until your time has come to expire; die.

Yes it's inconceivable why anyone would want to go to hell to die; burn. Yes I know the hardships you face in life because I've faced them. Sometimes I tell Lovey I would rather take my chances with death than stay with him. Life here on earth is hard, but it is infinitely and indefinitely harder in the spiritual realm if you are one of the wicked. There is no rest for the wicked in the spiritual realm. They cannot rest; they have to adhere to the laws of death. This is why some people are tormented in the living by death; some of these dead people and or spirits.

This life here on earth is **_THE LIFE OF CHOICE_** if this makes any sense to you. **_YOUR LIFE CHOICE THEN._**

This life is the choosing stage. Once you've made that choice, it is recorded and many of you cannot change this choice depending on your sins. Thus you were told, *"THE WAGES OF SIN IS DEATH BUT TRUTH IS LIFE EVERLASTING."* And I've constantly told you over and over again in some of my other books that, *"THE LIFE YOU LIVE HERE ON EARTH DETERMINES WHERE YOU GO IN THE AFTER LIFE; ONCE YOUR SPIRIT SHEDS THE FLESH."*

I've told you, know your sins and amend them because THERE IS NO WATER IN HELL. YOUR SPIRIT IS DEPENDANT ON WATER. IF YOUR SPIRIT DO NOT HAVE WATER IT DIES.

Your foundation begins with water so once the water in your spirit and or around your spirit depletes; the spirit is taken from you. Your time and or sand in your hourglass has and have run out then if that makes any sense to you. I know Lovey this is not the proper way of putting it but I have to try and let humanity over stand life and death. Life is truly not flesh but spirit, and I've told humanity this in some of the other books in the Michelle Jean Series of Books. Many say their isn't a God, but there is a God Lovey and that God is true and good life; You.

THERE IS A LIFE AND DEATH CHOICE LOVEY. YOU AND I KNOW THIS, BUT INSTEAD OF CHOOSING LIFE, BILLIONS HAVE AND HAS CHOSEN DEATH OVER LIFE. SO BECAUSE OF THIS CHOICE, BILLIONS CANNOT BE SAVED.

• • •

And yes you can say earth is a transition stage or phase. We are in transit for those who truly know. And yes this is on another level. And yes for those of you who fully and truly know, **it is wrong to say this (we are in transit) because there are no transitions in Life just LIFE.**

ALL ROYALS KNOW THEY ARE HELL BOUND BECAUSE OF THEIR NASTINESS AND INCESTUOUS BLOODLINE.

SO BECAUSE THEY ARE HELL BOUND, THEY HAD TO TAKE THEIR SUBJECTS TO HELL WITH THEM SO THAT THEY CAN RULE OVER YOU IN HELL. But none realize that in hell, no one can rule over you apart from death and the demons of hell. So to say you have to keep your bloodline pure truly good luck with that because no one's bloodline is pure in that sense; your thought of purity. **EVERY HUMAN BEING IS FROM THE SAME FOUNDATION AND THAT FOUNDATION IS BLACK.**

WHITES DID NOT GIVE RISE AND LIFE TO WHITES.

BLACK GAVE WHITES RISE AND LIFE BECAUSE YOU ARE FROM OUR FOUNDATION. YOU CAME FROM US, NOT THE OTHER WAY AROUND.

BLACKS GAVE BIRTH TO YOU BUT YET YOU HATE YOUR OWN BROTHER AND SISTER.

NO ONE ON THE FACE OF THIS PLANET CAN CLAIM ANOTHER FOUNDATION BECAUSE BLACK IS THE FOUNDATION OF ALL; THUS GOOD AND EVIL CRY OUT TO ALL FOR LIFE AND THAT LIFE IS LOVEY; ALLELUJAH AS HE IS OFTEN CALLED.

Say it let me blast you because this black foundation has nothing to do with the hue of man; humans. So don't come here with my blackness and whiteness bullshit or I will truly put you in your place.

You can hate all you want, but at the end of the day; you are truly locked out of Lovey's kingdom and you are hating self. Go to hell with your hatred because I know what death and the demons of hell are truly going to do with you. Stay caged with your hatred and sins because **like I've said, you created your own hell thus giving rise to your demons that haunt some of you in the living.**

NO ONE CAN SAY THEIR BLOODLINE IS TAINTED AND OR NOT PURE BECAUSE IT IS PURE. IT MATTERS NOT IF YOUR BLOODLINE IS OF LIFE OR DEATH; GOOD OR EVIL; IT IS PURE. *Lovey doesn't make anything tainted, so no one's bloodline can be tainted. And don't go there with the diseases of men.* **No one's true bloodline can be tainted and you all know this because no one can taint the spirit.** Don't go there with science either because science is not true on many levels. Man knows nothing of life and your true DNA; so they cannot tell you anything. ***Most of the shit that we are told are false; developed in laboratories to lie and deceive you.*** It's all a ponzi and or money making scheme to rob you and you all know this but yet think otherwise. ***If men knew life, they would have found the key to life already.*** *If men knew life, they would have known that your spirit is a reflection of the flesh and the flesh is a reflection of your spirit; your earthly DNA.* Thus man cannot find Lovey because they don't know where Lovey's kingdom and or abode is. So because of this, some tell you there is no God, some tell you, you have to accept this and this including death to see God. Death is a God and death kills. So when you die, you are going to see death not life, and this is if you have and has chosen death. ***If you have not chosen death you cannot die to see death; YOU HAVE TO LIVE TO SEE LOVEY; THUS WE HAVE A UPRIGHT AND A DOWNWARD TRIANGLE.*** Yes many people mock the upright triangle but dis a fi dem waterloo. They have to pay and pay shortly for their jokes and lies. ***Thus man and or humans know not life; hence they would have known the life that was given unto them. Come on now.***

Life is not death so live your life good and clean; true. Lovey cannot condemn you for your choice of death and he will never condemn you; I condemn you in his name.

You are a condemnation to life and of life and you must live your life as the condemned if you are wicked and evil.

Good don't trouble you, so truly do not trouble me.

IF YOUR DISEASED GOD IS YOUR CHOICE, KEEP HIM; YOUR DISEASED GOD THE FUCK OUT OF MY LIFE AND WORLD. DON'T COME INTO MY LAND WITH YOUR BULLSHIT OF NASTINESS BECAUSE I WILL EVICT YOUR ASS.

I TRULY DON'T NEED YOUR FILTH, SO DON'T COME AROUND ME WITH IT. KEEP YOUR FUCKING DISEASES BECAUSE I WILL PROTECT MY BELOVED OF TRUTH AT ALL COST. And fuck you with the weapons of mass destruction. I truly don't need them. I have the words and truth of Lovey and that's all I need. Thus we as black people need to wake the fuck up and do better for our self as a race and nation of people.

Any of you white people that fall under the banner of black say it so I can cuss your ass thoroughly. You need to wake the fuck up and know your truth of life. I've told you in some of my other books that some blacks are white; fall *under the banner of white; evil, and some whites are black; fall under the banner of black thus making your foundation truly black. <u>You are the ones to ignore your call with your hatred and hue; skin tone bullshit, colonization and slavery bullshit, greed and incestuous bullshit and so much more.</u> What you think black people based on your conception of hue were the only ones colonized and enslaved. <u>Your ass were colonized and enslaved too, so know the fucking truth of you; your blackness.</u>*

Just as Babylon don't like black people based on humanities conception of hue dem nuh like yu nieda. They will never like you because the majority of you are not of them. You are of black; fall under the black banner. ***<u>Why the hell do you think hue come into play?</u>***

You took up arms to fight with them without knowing that the ***WHITE RACE IS CURSED DUE TO THE FIGHTING THAT YOU AND OR THEY DO.***

<u>BLOOD MUST BE ON THEIR HANDS BECAUSE DEATH NEED BLOOD; THE DEATH OF A HUMAN LIFE TO STAY ALIVE. YOU THE WHITE RACE IS JUST A PAWN FOR SIN; SATAN BECAUSE SATAN WAS NOT ONE OF YOU. SATAN WAS A FULL BRED</u>

BABYLONIAN AND MANY OF YOU FOLLOW HIM
TO YOUR GRAVES. Many of you know this also
but instead of doing right you do wrong.

I've shown you the blackness and or the darkness of your evils; sins, thus you have some that are white and some that are black in hue.

I've shown you and told you that our skin tone and or hue is shit because both skin tone represent DEATH; PHYSICAL AND SPIRITUAL DEATH WITH WHITE; WHITE HUE BEING FINAL DEATH IN THE SPIRITUAL REALM. EVERYONE DIES AS WHITE DRESSED IN WHITE IN THE SPIRITUAL REALM AND IT MATTERS NOT YOUR COLOUR; HUE HERE ON EARTH. This is the way we all die if your life here on earth is evil; filled with sin. Good cannot die; only wickedness and evil can and will die. BLACK DEATH JUST HAND YOU OVER TO WHITE DEATH PERIOD. So truly know your life and sins here on earth because I've told you, the life you save might just be your own.

KNOW THAT LONG AFTER DEATH IS GONE, LIFE WILL STILL BE HERE. SO DEATH IS TRULY NOT GREATER THAN LIFE, LIFE IS GREATER THAN DEATH.

So go ahead and hate me all you want because I know and see the backlash and hatred I am going to receive over social media. I know the hatred that will spew and swirl and frankly I don't give a damn. You have the truth so save your fucking life. I don't want or need your soul and or spirit. I've told you, true love cannot hurt; it can only save. ***True love must make a good, clean and positive way for the people and or chosen few of Lovey.*** So if you want to hate me fuck you because I'm already saved and safe with Lovey. Like I said, I know hell and I truly don't want you to go there. And to say I am saved by Jesus truly good luck to you because I know otherwise.

DEATH IS YOUR CHOICE SO FUCKING DIE. WHY THE HELL SHOULD I LAY MY LIFE OR ANYONE LAY THEIR LIFE ON THE LINE FOR IGNORANT AND STUPID PEOPLE?

People that have no fucking sense when it comes to life and death. You made the choice to sin, so why the fuck should I die or anyone die for you? What makes your life so fucking important that someone should just come and give up theirs for you? Your shit isn't gold; it stinks like the rest of us. So bleep you. I can't save you when I'm death so wake the fuck up and save you. You are your saving grace also. Death takes life; death does not save life ***AND I REFUSE TO CONVERT OR CHANGE ANYONE FROM THEIR DEATH CHOICE. THIS IS YOUR GOOD WILL TO DIE, SO I AM STEPPING ASIDE AND LEAVING YOUR ASS TO DIE ESPECIALLY YOU IN THE BLACK RACE. UNNU TOO FOOL FOOL AN DUNKCYA.***

Unnu claim unnu a di first creation ***BUT YET THE FIRST CREATION DO NOT KNOW THE FULL TRUTH OF THEM; HOW THEY CAME INTO BEING.***

UNNU CLAIM SEY UNNU A DI FIRST CREATION, BUT YET HAVE NO DEFINED AND DEFINITE LANGUAGE OF YOUR OWN.

UNNU CLAIM SEY UNNU A DI FIRST CREATION, BUT CAN'T TELL ME WHICH LAND THE FIRST CREATION CAME FROM.

UNNU CLAIM SEY UNNU A DI FIRST CREATION, BUT YET KNOW NOT YOUR TRUE LIFE STORY, HERITAGE AND DESCENT; CULTURE.

Unnu come from backa wall an backa bush; thus unnu nuh ha sense fi noa sey crap was infiltrated in the black man's world, and the books of men were created to make the lots of you look stupid and ignorant; fool fool. Like ole people sey, ***WRITE UNNU NAME PON PIECE A BULLA CAKE AN UNNU GWAP IT DUNG WITHOUT KNOWING SEY UNNU NAME WRITE PON IT." AND SO SAID SO DONE BECAUSE UNNU GWAP DUNG DI SHIT WEY MAN WRITE AN GI UNNU AN UNNU SEY A GOOD FOOD.***

Look humuch a unnu kill fi religion and politricks (politics).

Look humuch a unnu tun gense Lovey with unnu bullshit.

Look humuch a unnu teach unnu pickney dem di same bullshit.

Look humuch a unnu man an oman; unnu owna people gi all manner of devil worship and death tu, an unnu run wid dem anna praise dem without knowing sey, unnu hell bound; name is written in the book of death because of this; your foolish and selfish; greedy actions. Thus Demarco tell unnu humuch a unnu sell out fi paypa. Yes nuff a unnu batty tun up, an nuff a unnu pay death (Obeah Man an Oman, Science Man an Oman fi tun dung an tek life.

Yes go ahead and sey it; thus I can say yet again, listen to wey Demarco tell di SELL OUTS DEM INNA DI RAZZ ATTACK RIDDIM MIX.

You can save yourself if you want to, so fucking do it. <u>LOVEY IS NOT GOING TO LET HIS GOOD UP GOOD UP PEOPLE DEM DEAD FI UNNU. LOVEY WOULD NEVER DO THIS, BUT DEAD WOULD.</u> Not to save you but to kill you. So truly good luck with your living for death bullshit.

MANY SO CALLED WHITE PEOPLE HATED THE BLACK RACE AND STILL DO TODAY. SO THEIR ANCESTORS COLONIZED BLACK NATIONS (BABYLONIAN NATIONS EXCLUDED), CHANGED OUR BOOKS OF TRUTH, GAVE US THEIR

NASTINESS, NASTY CULTURE AND DEMONIC WAYS, GAVE US THEIR BOOKS TO CONDEMN AND BRING US AND YOU SHAME LOVEY; BOOKS WE READ FROM UNTIL THIS DAY.

THEY MADE US INTO SLAVES AND CALL US SLAVES; CALL US APES AND MONKIES; NOT HUMAN BUT A SUB HUMAN SPECIES.

All this you allow Lovey. So how can truth prevail if you allow wickedness of sin to constantly teach us their lies and nasty ways?

What is the point of asking me to write you a book not once but twice and nothing is being done to vindicate the good and true of this earth and universe?

Until this day; when you come with the truth to teach our own cleanliness and truth they hate you, talk all manner of shit against you, sell you out and want to kill you. We've been so conditioned to accept this book (so called holy bible) that we would rather die than change our filthy and disgusting ways. We accept lies and kill the truth then turn around and complain to you; cry wolf. *Lovey you can no longer listen to heathens that sell you out to Sin; Satan.*

We refuse the truth now truly close the door to the black race come on now. I am tired of the bullshit we and or they accept come on now.

Further, I am tired of quarreling with you and crying wolf. I truly need stability with us. I cannot go on this way anymore thus forgive me for yesterday (October 27, 2015). I came to you harsh and brutal and it was truly not fair to you. My son is truly not listening. You cannot say you want to be this in the future and instead of building yourself for the future educationally, you are tearing yourself down. Education is important to me Lovey, but it seems education is truly not important to many in the black race based on hue; Babylonians excluded. I truly don't know Lovey because I truly don't know why you have to fall to rise. Some people never rise; they are still down and some are dead. If you are getting life the easy way filled with truth and positivity then take it; run with it and build yourself. Don't look back. Get rid of the negative influences in your life and move forward in a positive and true way.

Yes I have hope Lovey and wish you would give me the easy way in a positive and true way so that I can truly live without the negative forces that is in my home and that surround me as well. I need my life to be filled with positivity because I cannot battle you anymore for the good of my children. They don't want to have ambition to truly learn and make better choices and or positive life choices then so be it. I have to go my way just like you. It's time now for me to stop beating you up and using you as my beating stick due to my children and the actions of others. It's time to reconcile with you in a good way; thus I truly have to put away this fierce anger that is inside of me. You are not deserving of my anger and it's not fair for me to be angry at you anymore for the crap my children and others do. So truly forgive me for yesterday and see with me because in truth, I can't leave you and I cannot let my children let me lose my place with you. Yes it's hard and I thank you for bearing with me and sticking it out with me.

LOVEY, ZION FELL; HER TIME HAS AND HAVE EXPIRED, SO LET ZION'S NASTY PEOPLE GO. THEY REFUSE THE TRUTH, SO TRULY LET THEM GO. YOU CANNOT CONTINUOUSLY TRY TO SAVE PEOPLE THAT TRULY DO NOT WANT SAVING COME ON NOW. They refuse you and accept death without thinking of the hell they are going to have to pay. So truly let them go. You cannot keep trailing behind them and say accept life and or me. You are no one's bitch come on now. Have some true respect for you and truly love you because love is not truth and you know this.

It seems as if we as black people cannot truly learn because we've turned from your truth and accepted the devil's own. WE AS ***BLACK PEOPLE PREACH AND TEACH FROM THIS NASTY BOOK CALLED THE HOLY BIBLE FOR WHAT!! WHERE IS OUR GOOD AND TRUE BOOK LOVEY?***

WHERE IS OUR GOOD AND TRUE HOLY BIBLE THAT IS TRULY OF YOU; YOUR GOODNESS AND TRUTH?

WE SAY WE LOVE YOU, BUT YET HAVE NO TRUE BOOKS FROM YOU. HOW CAN WE SAY WE LOVE YOU BUT YET CANNOT LISTEN TO YOU? HOW CAN WE SAY WE LOVE YOU BUT CANNOT HEAR YOU?

Yes these books are there but they are ignored by my own; so I have to stop giving my own books now. I have to go another route. I have to go out there and do my job; save another nation because my own truly do not want saving from what I can see. Many have come before me preaching and teaching the truth, but instead of accepting the truth, we sell them out (the truth out) like I've said above and I am truly tired of it.

WE BASK IN THE NASTINESS OF THEM (SIN) AND THEIR CONDEMNED BOOK AND BOOKS THUS CONDEMNING OUR SELF AND LOCKING OUR SELF OUT OF YOUR GOOD AND TRUE KINGDOM LOVEY. WE ALSO TEACH OUR CHILDREN THESE NASTINESS THUS CARRYING ON THE NASTY AND FILTHY TRADITIONS OF MEN, MEN THAT ARE CONDEMNED.

MAN MADE SURE WE HAD THEIR BIBLE – THEIR SO CALLED HOLY BOOK THAT THEY SAY IS FROM YOU; DIVINELY INSPIRED. NOW TELL ME, HOW CAN MAN'S NASTY BOOK BE DIVINELY INSPIRED IF IT'S FILLED WITH FILTH; DEATH?

MEN USED YOU BIG TIME LOVEY AND NOW THEY ARE LAUGHING AT HUMANITY BECAUSE THEY WON. THEY GAVE SATAN AND OR EVIL AND OR DEATH THE ACCESS THEY NEEDED TO DECEIVE AND KILL. THEY'VE TAKEN ALL FROM YOU LOVEY INCLUDING YOUR DIGNITY.

MEN SACRIFICED HUMANS GLOBALLY FOR DOMINANCE AND CONTROL AND YOU COULDN'T STOP THIS.

So as Satan and his people grew in strength and power you Lovey became weak and powerless; helpless to do anything for your good and true people. Thus you are left on the sidelines while humanity praise and worship Egyptian deities and man himself.

We lost you and you are nowhere to be found here on earth because no one truly wants you. You are not recognized; thus your people turned against you and accepted things that were not from you. You cannot blame man; humans for this Lovey because you lost; humans globally sold you out to death and all you can do is look on with your head bowed down in shame.

Thus I ask you yet again. What was the purchase of creating it all for man to come and destroy it all?

And please truly do not tell me about hell because humans do not care about hell. Earth has become the cesspool of sin and evil thus man carry on with their wickedness daily. No one thinks of the consequences thus sin; wickedness and evil is glamorized by billions globally. Just look at the internet and some video games and you will see.

● ● ●

Read some of those horror and occult books that are out there and you will see.

Look at the way man; humans kill each other for politics and religion.

Look at how humans hate each other due to politics and religion.

Look at how evil and negative energy surrounds the earth as well as consume the earth. So tell me Lovey, who are you truly?

It's over now. Truly over because no one can stop sin. You can't because sin and or wicked and evil men control the global empires ***and the subjects within society have to comply with their lies lest they be killed; made an example of.*** Like I said, you allow this nonsense to happen because when you truly look at it, ***men are not peaceful beings. They seek control and dominance and it matters not who they kill to have this control and dominance.***

Look at the lives of many citizens globally that are muzzled by these insane men that say they run countries. Tell me Lovey, what freedom do some have?

What freedom do they have?

Politics and religion take away your freedom hence no one lives in a free society. Politics and religion was designed to keep you hungry. They were also designed to keep you imprisoned because if you cannot buy food or find food, you have to go out there and steal to get it.

You have to break the laws of truth and sin yourself in order to live. This is the system humans created for humans to stray from you. When we sin Lovey, you leave us and evil knew this but man could not reject evil. They accepted evil then write their books of lies and give them to humanity and say these lies are from you; divinely inspired. We as humans fail to realize that we do not have to live under the lies of sin. We are more than capable and can live true without sin. Sin dirty us and because of this dirt we cannot find you; you leave us.

So tell me Lovey, how do you truly feel in knowing all of this?

How do you feel to know that you of yourself cannot stop the lies of men; humans when it comes to you?

Now tell me, what was the point of you asking me to write you a book when you know the lies and deceit of men is widely accepted and truth is rejected?

Was the purpose of truth not defeated long ago with the lies and deceit of men?

Evil infiltrated our home and space; took control of your name and people and no matter what you've done throughout the course of history; man's history you failed. Evil made sure you could not win because evil controls society globally. Yes I know you still have some of your people but Lovey; look at the history and life of us humans until this day.

WE'VE FORGOTTEN THAT EVIL HAD 24000 YEARS TO LIE AND DECEIVE. WITHIN OR IN THOSE 24000 YEARS WE AS HUMANS HAD THE OPPORTUNITY TO REFUSE AND OR REJECT EVIL AND COME BACK TO LIFE, BUT BILLIONS REFUSED YOUR CALL LOVEY UNTIL THIS DAY.

__24000 years was not for the devil alone.__ Those 24000 were also for man and humankind; those who have lost their way. I know this and you know this, but instead of humans choosing goodness and truth for self; we let others convince us to choose death over good and true life.

We give up our place with you for a place with death and it's truly not fair; it's sad. ***LIFE DID NOT SAY DEATH BECAUSE LIFE CANNOT SAY DEATH. LIFE KNOWS NOT DEATH. DEATH IS THE ONLY ONE THAT CAN SAY DEATH BECAUSE IN TRUE TRUTH, DEATH KNOWS NOT LIFE, THUS DEATH CANNOT LIVE A TRUE AND GOOD LIFE; IT CAN ONLY DIE.***

Now tell me, what good can I do?

• • •

What good can I do for you?

How can I correct the wrongs that were done to you?

How do we as humans pick up the pieces and move on from the lies that were written by men, and yes some woman and children?

LOVEY, HOW CAN YOU LOOK TO ANY MAN; MALE AND SAY, WELL DONE WHEN IT COMES TO THEM?

HOW CAN YOU LOOK TO ANY MAN; MALE AND SAY, YOU ARE MY CHILD?

HOW CAN YOU TRUST ANY MAN; MALE LOVEY?
HOW CAN YOU TRUST A MALE LOVEY?

You are God alone but yet man; males tell so much lies on you. Women do this also because *THEY PREACH FROM THE SAME LYING AND DECEITFUL BOOK AS THEIR MALE COUNTERPARTS.*

Lovey why allow this?

Why play and or go along with the games of men?

Do you not hurt?

Do you not cry?

No, I should not ask you if you are hurt because I know you are and I know that you cry also. All you've given humanity in truth and humanity has and have turned against you by siding with sin and death against you. Now we are looking for a saving grace and expecting you to save us. But how can you truly save us Lovey when we lie and sin against you? We did not choose good and true life here on earth so how can you truly save humanity?

I've told you, if I was the saving grace of humanity I would save no one who is wicked and evil and I truly mean this.

Why should a wicked and evil person be saved when they do all to keep humanity broken and away from you?

Only you know Lovey.
Only you know.

This life is corrupt; corrupted by humans.
There are no safe havens anymore.

To me you're not a fair God in all that you do. You truly do not care for all; thus you've neglected the life and truth of Mother Earth. *__Yes you are male and female, but from a male perspective you keep the lies flowing and going because Males are the demons of this world.__ They divide and conquer; control, steal and tell lies to keep them satisfied. They care not for this world and earth; they keep evil going, thus humans die whilst taking the earth with them more and more.* All this could be stopped but as Bob said, "nothing can stop them now." The damage has been done; thus billions are hell bound and they truly do not know it. Evil told humanity what they were going to do and none in humanity listened. Therefore, the more we sin the further you Lovey get from us.

We seek you but yet cannot find.

Some say they've found, but I know for a fact they have not found you. All they've found is the God of Death; War.

No human being can sojourn with you in an unclean state and society and this humanity cannot figure out.

No human being can or will find you if they are of the church; religion because you are not a religion; you are good and true life, God alone.

No human being can or will find you if they are of the political arena. They join forces with death, thus they have to put money away for death so that death take the lives of others including their own. Further, politics is war because man do pit countries against countries thus the enmity and strife between them. Therefore, Death and or Aries will forever walk with man and take at will because of wicked and evil men globally. Wicked and Evil men that seek to control; kill whist using your name as a bargaining chip; tool. **_So_**

<u>because they have no peace and truth in their lives; their citizens cannot have peace and truth in their lives.</u>

They are filled with rage and love, not truth and true love. They deceive and kill; let their people live in hell with them.

So because they have no truth and true love for this earth, their people and the land they live in; they sacrifice earth, their people and the land they live in; thus the blood that is infinitely and indefinitely in and on their hands.

<u>Their way is hell so they take earth, their people and the land they live in to hell with them. So there is no peace in the hearts men, just war, brutality and bloodshed. They kill for a place in hell thus there is no true peace here on earth.</u>

No citizen is true to the land they live in either Lovey, because they see and know all these things but refuse to change self and land for the better. None seek you in truth Lovey nor do they pray to you for truth and true peace in their land and home. None see the greater good of them; thus evil surround the earth and wicked and evil men and women including children govern this earth. <u>Faada an mumma (madda) wicked soh pickney come wicked tu.</u>

We all know the time of Noah and instead of preserving life, we take all from life including self. Now the time has come when mass destruction will be on earth and no messenger can stop this. I certainly don't want to. Let the destruction begin because humans live for greed and selfishness; thus it is our greed and selfishness that is going to take billions to hell to face that hell there. As humans we know better but refuse to do better.

We want it all and it matters not how we get it as long as we get it. But in the end all that we kill to get, steal to get must catch up to us. We must pay for our sins ***AND LOVEY IS NOT GOING TO LET THE NEXT MAN WOMAN OR CHILD PAY THE PENALTY FOR YOUR SINS.***

LOVEY CANNOT MAKE SOMEONE DIE FOR YOUR SINS. HE CANNOT SACRIFICE ANYONE TO DEATH FOR YOU BECAUSE I'VE TOLD YOU ABOVE, LIFE KNOWS NOT DEATH.

NO ONE CAN DIE FOR YOUR SINS BECAUSE WE WERE TOLD, "THE WAGES OF SIN IS DEATH."

YOU COMMIT YOUR SINS AND YOU ARE THE ONE TO PAY FOR THEM *NOT THE NEXT MAN OR WOMAN INCLUDING CHILD.*

I did not sin for you. I cannot sin for you because you are you and I am me. I have my own cross to bare and you cannot bare it for me. My cross could be heavier than yours. Now I ask you this. ***WHY WOULD YOU WANT TO***

CARRY MY CROSS FOR ME KNOWING THAT YOU ARE GOING TO DIE? If you had one cross (sin) to bare and I have one million crosses to carry and bare, why would you want to add my million crosses to your cross and have one million and one crosses. **_YOU NOW HAVE ONE MORE SIN AND OR CROSS THAN ME; SO YOU ARE GOING TO STAY IN HELL LONGER THAN ME._**

Now what if your child had two good fruits on his or her plate and they said, God, Lovey; because I truly love my father and mother, give them one each of my good fruit; you cannot be saved because you took on the burden of another man or woman including child's sin thus your one million and one sins. **_YOU GAVE UP YOUR PLACE WITH LOVEY SO DEATH MUST TO TAKE YOU TO HELL WITH THEM._** So your child's good became naught to you; null and void because their good could not save you. You took away you from them and Lovey and you have no one to blame but you. **_GOODNESS DOES NOT MEAN GIVING UP YOUR RIGHT AND PLACE WITH LOVEY FOR SOMEONE ELSE._** You can share what you have, but it does not mean give all of you to the next person when they are not deserving of it. This is what's happened to many black civilizations throughout the course of history and or time. Many have and has lost their place with Lovey thus I've told you time and time again that, *"HELL IS FULL OF BLACK PEOPLE AND RECRUITING MORE."*

• • •

Many black kingdoms did give up their life to join the ranks of death; thus Islam is so predominant in Africa. ***Blacks did accept Islam after Lovey forbid us to go back into this realm.*** *Islam is not peace it's spiritual death because this way of life became so dirty that Lovey has and have turned his back on everyone and everything in the Islamic Kingdom.* IslamF. ***Thus it's written and it's a known fact among the true Jews that no Jew can cohabitate, marry, procreate and get involved with anyone of the Islamic Kingdom.*** JEWS, THE TRUE JEWS MUST CONTINUE TO KEEP THEMSELVES SACRED AND TRUE SO THAT TRUE LIFE CAN COME BACK TO EARTH EVENTUALLY.

The laws of Men and or Man do not concern a true Jew.

They are not governed by the laws of men; they are governed by the law and laws of Lovey, God.

So because many black lands; people have and has changed their name and language and accepted death's language and name; they cannot be saved. *THEY ARE MORE THAN INFINITELY AND INDEFINITELY LOCKED OUT OF LOVEY'S KINGDOM AND ABODE.* Thus, ***"HELL IS FULL OF BLACK PEOPLE AND RECRUITING MORE."***

And to be honest with you, from what's happening in this world no one truly cares. As my son says he does not believe in God and who can blame him. Is God not shoved down our throats by everyone?

● ● ●

Today my world is different due to the fact that all I see is wickedness and control by evil men and women including children. Nothing has changed over the centuries because Lovey and or God permit this evil to happen. I cannot comprehend why he would do this?

Yes I know the sins of man due to Will; choice. He gave us Will and maybe this was what he was trying to tell me when he showed me his first creating looking like Will Smith. We have the will to choose good and evil and many have and has chosen evil will over good; thus we've become ugly in all that we do.

WILL IS NOT BEAUTIFUL IN MY SIGHT; IT'S UGLY. THUS THE UGLINESS OF SPIRIT WHEN IT COMES TO HUMANS.

Yes the spirit is ugly and the mindset disturbed today but in truth, I truly do not care. I truly do not give a damn what Lovey thinks hence I truly hate October. It's filled with disappointment and anger for me so far. Nothing positive has or have happened for me in this month. It's depressing and filled with anger and shame. Yes there are other things happening in this world but in truth, today I truly do not care who want to live or who want to die. I truly don't care about death or who death takes. The lives of billions are truly not my worry because as humans, we are the ones to give up our lives to men and women including children that are not bleeping deserving of it. I will not take myself out of this because in truth I gave me away to Lovey only to realize that you cannot give someone and or a God that have no true love your truth and all.

No people, I am looking at the world on a whole and I surf the net (internet) for which I have to stop doing and all I see is pain and confusion.

I see hatred and shame.

I see sin all over again due to content and language; what some people do.

I see political divide.

I see war and strife.
Diseases
War machines.

I see death all over again and I have to stop this.

I have to truly think because this life here on earth stinks. I see men at the head of their countries leading their people into hell but yet the people are powerless to help self. ***Maybe it's me, but I cannot fathom why we as people let evil and ruthless people govern our lives?***

Why do we add their sins to our sins and create more sins for our self?

I cannot fathom the concept of dictatorship and pain. *How can you say you govern your people but yet keep them hungry?*

How can you as a leader say you love your people, but yet massacre them and take away their fundamental rights to life if they don't do as you say; follow you? This is jacked up and fucked up come on now. Who the fuck are you to take my right and rights to a decent and peaceful life from me?

Lovey don't do it, so why the fuck am I letting you do this bullshit to me?

You are not my mother and father; creator. No, I want my life back; thus I am tossing you to the side and living my life the way Lovey want and need me to. I will not participate in your bullshit because you are not me, we are truly not related and if we were, I would disown you as a family member and walk away from you.

My life is not built on dictatorship and control; domination.

Why the hell should I go to hell and die because of you? You shit and piss the same way I do.

There is absolutely nothing great about you, but yet you take my freedom from me. I'm walking away from you and living right; right by me and life, not you. I want and need to live. I refuse to die with you and I refuse to live by your dictatorship ways. NO ONE LIKES TO BE CONTROLLED. I DID NOT GIVE YOU CONTROL OVER MY LIFE, SO WHY THE FUCK ARE YOU CONTROLLING ME AND TELLING ME WHAT TO DO?

You are overstepping your boundaries because you're not God: Lovey. You can't control your life but because you have authority and or were elected to office you feel like you can control me and I'm the fool to let you.

YOU CAN'T SAVE ME. ALL YOU ARE DOING IS RUINING ME AND I REFUSE TO LET YOU CONTINUE TO RUIN ME. YOUR HEART IS FILTHY AND DIRTY THUS YOU RULE WITH YOUR FILTHY AND DIRTY SELF; HEART.

You impose laws that are ill fit for any human being. <u>You're fucking ugly and that is why no one likes you.</u>

You're a bully that has NO HUMAN CONTENT OR CHARACTER. Thus the demons that live in you and surrounds you. <u>You are surrounded by like manner men and women including children; thus you kill to get what you want.</u> Anyone that oppose you, you kill. YOU LIVE A NASTY LIFESTYLE IN YOUR HOME BUT YET IN PUBLIC YOU PRETEND TO BE CLEAN.

YOU PRETEND TO BE HOLY. WELL FUCK YOU BECAUSE I SEE THE DIRTINESS OF YOU; THUS YOUR PISS AND SHIT STINKS JUST LIKE ANYONE ELSE.

YOU'RE A CONDEMNATION OF LIFE AND SPIRIT; THUS HELL HAS YOUR NAME AND NUMBER LITERALLY.

Your children as a leader go to the best school outside and inside your country. They wear designer clothing and get all they want from you, but yet ordinary citizens and children go hungry for food and water; shelter; their basic need; necessities of life. Yes this grieves me to know that this is happening globally because of Men; our so called leaders.

Am I down on Lovey?

Yes, thus I refer him to a man now. He's unjust because he permits this despite him giving us will. ***YES HE'S SHOWN ME THE WILL OF MAN IS UGLY BUT WITH HIM SHOWING ME THIS, IT TRULY DOES NOT EASE MY PAIN AND ANGER.***

When you look at the resources of this earth and the way some people are living here on earth, I want to hate him Lovey. No, I am not going to hide my conscience. I refuse to with him and to him including you. People are living in fear and in poverty because of their leaders, Male and Female including Monarchy and I'm to be happy with Lovey for this? No, I am truly not happy and wish he was never born on this day.

Yes I said it because it's truly painful to see what human beings have and has become over the centuries. I hurt to know that human beings kill each other. We find ways to eradicate other people from the face of this earth.

We say God gave us laws to live by as written by Men, but yet every law given to us we break. We are not to kill but yet we kill.

Humans create diseases to infect and kill other people. This is their so called population control and ethnic cleansing.

Humans create war machines, bombs and ammunition, guns and put it in the hands of their people and tell them go to war and fight against this land. You're protecting your land.

Our LEADERS and or the leaders OF OUR COUNTRY (land) TURN US (THEIR) CITIZENS INTO MURDERERS and THIEVES.

THEY SEND THEIR CITIZENS ON THE BATTLEFIELD TO KILL ANOTHER HUMAN BEING THUS VIOLATING THE COMMANDMENT OF GOD; "THOU SHALT NOT KILL," as written by men in their so called holy bible.

So tell me, how can anyone be happy in a world filled with murderers and thieves; people who kill at will to keep death alive here on earth?

So yes my spirit is different and I have to ask what is the purpose of God?

Isn't God a fraud?

Isn't God based on lies; the distortion of Egyptian facts and truths?

Did Babylon not invade Egypt and distort the facts to include them as well as suit them?

Did Babylon not deceive humanity?

So how can we including me continue to say we believe and or know God when the God given to us is truly not real?

Are we not living and dwelling on false hope?
Are we not condemned to hell?

So which God do you serve?

I know Lovey is real people but on this day, he's not real to me and I truly want and need to leave his fold. I truly don't care if I lose him on this day. I cannot find any truth in him because of the shit and mess that's happening in this world. Thus this book is my heart to heart with him. Well her to me. I truly don't want to know the Him part of him anymore because of what males are doing here on earth.

● ● ●

They spread lies and say this is what He God wants. ***Thus the lies of HIM GOD has shaped the lives of billions on this earth.*** So no more HIM for me on this day because there is absolutely *NO GOOD OR TRUE DESIRE IS IN ME FOR THE HIM SIDE OF LOVEY.* Therefore, she said God kills and now I know she is correct because Death is a God also. Death kills but good and true life cannot kill. I cannot over stand why Lovey would allow wicked and evil men and women including some children to kill.

Yes people I know the difference between life and death; good and evil. I know Lovey, therefore I have to go to Lovey with all my troubles; problems. I cannot go to anyone else but Lovey because I did make Lovey a part of my life all around.

Earth is a killing field for humans because war never cease and no one is asking themselves why?

No leader is asking self why?

Why do we have to fight?
Why did these people become my enemy?

What have this land done to my land that I have to fight against them; kill their people?

Well they invaded my country and killed my people and because of this I have to fight against them you are saying.

But is it an eye for an eye?

No, that's a stupid question because it is an eye for an eye even for me. ***But I will not take up arms against you. I refuse to.*** Hell is there thus I say and tell Lovey, if I am the saving grace for humanity, I will not save anyone that is wicked and evil, nor will I save certain lands and their people. So yes it's good to know that there is an App (HELL) for wicked and evil people and spirits of this world and universe.

So if He Lovey wants, he can send someone else to save them (those I refuse to save) but I refuse to save them. I would rather spit on the earth and sin myself than save these nations and people (those I refuse to save). ***The good ones I leave alone because good cannot take away from good. Therefore Lovey knows it's up to him to keep the good ones safe and send someone else to save them (those that are good that are in the land and lands I refuse to save). I will not take away the right of good from good. This is just wrong on my part. Thus life here on earth is truly confusing for me. I truly hate life right now because of the injustice here on earth.***

How can She Lovey, just stand aside and look?

How can a mother watch the ones she's given birth to die like this at the hands of men; wicked and evil humans? How can She God side with a wicked and evil Man; Male God?

Yes I know the abuse, how Men are abusive but what about your good and true escape Mother?

Why let earth become the cesspool and dung of the universe because of wicked and evil humans?

How could he give Man; the Devil 24000 years of life to deceive and kill?

Did you not feel the pain of giving birth?

SO WHY LET MEN; A MALE TAKE YOUR GLORY AND TRUTH FROM YOU?

Why live haggard out and in pain like me because of HIM?

What man is worth it my darling, what man is worth it?

We trust them but they fail us. Can't protect us because they have no true life in them just death. This is why they give humans death to live by.

This is why they kill because they constantly want control and if they don't have control; they imprison you and or kill you. They are living a good life because they rape the system of it's wealth as well as rape their citizens of their wealth and dignity; fundamental human right and rights.

● ● ●

Behind closed doors they bang every whore imaginable because whores are bedded on a different night.

They have power so they can do whatever they want to.

They can buy you if they want to; sell you if they want to.

You become their prostitute and possession because they own you and you have to do their dirty will; job. You become their blow fish and electric eel; the piranhas of the sea; waters; their rivers of water.

They feed you all the lies they want and you have to accept these lies because they run the country; are in control.

Some don't care if your child lay dead on the street as long as it's not theirs everything is okay.

Some rape the economy because billions of dollars is diverted from the government's bank account into their personal offshore bank accounts. Some have many; thus ensuring their whores, wife, wives and children including bastard children they have while married is kept financially secure for life.

<u>It's all about them and not the true security and life of the land they live in and or call home.</u> Ah yes, the friends and foes are well compensated too.

Many friends were given funds by them; thus the larger than large life some of the friends live.

The many mansions, wild sexual and drug filled parties.

The enclaves, oh man the enclaves they have just to keep their peeps happy and alive. Thus they buy friends, have many escorts; paid thrills.

Ah the life of the wicked and evil. Many envy them but in the end, why envy someone or anyone that hath no soul; cannot live beyond the grave?

Ah yes, _the new world order of the super rich trillionaires._ Billionaires are pasay now. It's now the world of the trillionaires; thus real money is the talk and the billionaires will have no say; have to walk. One does own it all and what will humanity do now?

As Bob said, check out the real situation because no one can stop them now.

Man's new world order is here and the devil must reign over their people because humanity made it so.

Man; humans bowed down to the devil and made death their king and queen. So truly good luck to humanity because hell is truly going to make you pay. Hell is truly here and no one can stop this hell. Yes it's October 28th 2015 and I am toggling between dates. I don't know if this dream had to do with me watching Jamaican fights on the internet yesterday, or if it's the fact that I went totally ballistic on Lovey for my son missing school in lieu of work.

Yes he wants to make money and not bother me for money, but Fam, why further jeopardize your schooling? You are down so many credits already that you won't graduate on time.

You don't wake up in time for school and it's a constant battle with you for you to wake up.

You say you want to be this in the future but yet you are not making a positive effort to be future ready. So how can I trust you to excel when you of yourself has set yourself up for failure? Yes I know this is your life but don't go backwards; move forward come on now.

If you want life and or good for yourself, make good and true; positive and clean life choices come on now.

So I don't know Fam, but this morning I kept dreaming and seeing black people; children and or young people in barren lands. The lands were so barren and dry nothing grew. ***This is all I could see over and over again.***

Storms came upon black lands with barrenness. No growth were in these lands, but dry dirt. So I truly do not know when it comes to black lands globally. People, I am so disgusted at our young children that I truly don't care about them on this day. On one of the videos I saw, this young girl was disrespecting her father and this lady had to say no, this is your father you can't disrespect him like that. I quarrel with Lovey thus I told you above I truly have to stop. In all that I quarrel with him for, I now know that I am being disrespectful because he truly do not deserve it despite me making him my beating stick and all. I cannot quarrel with him for the betterment of my children and others and I've told you this above. ***Lovey did not make the choices for them; they made it (the choice) for self. So for me to constantly quarrel with him Lovey is truly wrong on my part.***

In the video you had some people saying the father should not do that, hit his daughter in public like that and to the way di gyal was going on, I said he should wap har, shi too damn rude. Shi a pass har place. If your father is saying go into the car, go and don't gi attitude. Yu a nuh oman, you're his child and despite how you feel about your father in the household, ***do not take it on street and disrespect him.*** I know what it's like to be disrespected in public by your child. You feel shame and embarrassed, and in the society that I am in, you cannot hit your child and or children in public. Some kids and or children tell you, if you hit them dem a goh call 911; like a di police or government did lay and get them. Yes I know some parents go overboard with the hitting and some brutalize and abuse their children and this is unfortunate but in truth, you cannot spare the rod and spoil the child in certain things. You have to discipline them. My grandmother wasn't fraide fi discipline wi and mi noh fraide fi discipline mi pickney dem. Dem old now and when they are wrong I tell them they are wrong. I can't drape dem up but mi sure as hell can cuss dem and tell dem sey dem noh ha ambition when dem truly rattle my cage and piss mi off. Yes you can spoil your child because I do spoil mine in a lot of ways. And no there are no underlying tones here. Abuse is abuse and I will not take away from abuse but that gyal needed to be disciplined because she was disrespectful and rude to her father, thus her sins will be hers to bare when she gets older. She had better seek the forgiveness of her father because trust mi, di retribution wey a goh face har; she is going to wish and pray she did not do that to her father. Trust mi, di sins wey fall pan har, whoa Allelujah; di demons of hell is going to make her pay. Allelujah. Wow, glory. Truss mi, if shi noh guh mad she lucky because someone was on her side; favoured her.

Fi di fourteen year old wey stan up an cuss anna fight di older woman, where is your respect. Yu a leggo beese? You do not stand up and cuss or even fight your elders. Yu nuh ha home training?

Yu mumma an pupa naah raise yu right? Obviously not for you to be arguing with your elder. Soh nuh betta barrel nuh betta herring. And no one had better look at me to the cussing that I do in some of these books. Some of you need to be told in a harsh way the truth. You cannot do wrongs and expect someone to come along and give you right for the wrongs you have done come on now.

Fi yu di faada wey bax dung yu baby for not wanting her tea, I truly hope when the hands of time hit yu, an yu caane goh and nuh waane drink fiyu tea or or eat your food and yu get bax inna yu face, yu memba wey yu du to yu pickney. As for yu di mumma, hog lacka yu shouldn't ha pickney. ***You are worthless and without conscience.*** I would not and would never call you a mother. You're a fucking disgrace to all woman globally. No father should bax dung dem pickney an pick dem up by the hair just because dem nuh want tea. Some children are not hungry first thing in the morning and you cannot force them to eat or drink if they are not ready to. Every child's stomach is made differently when it comes to eating and hunger. You as a mother should know this and know better. That child will tell you when they are hungry, but den yu a hog and not of the human race. And not even hog treat dem pickney di way your husband and or baby faada treat that child.

You the black race have become so disgusting that some a unnu see men beating their wives or girlfriend and film it whilst laughing and putting it up on YouTube.

Yes I saw di man beating di oman with har pickney inna har han an di pickney drop. People walked by seeing this man abusing this woman and did nothing, not even call the police. You who was videotaping this shit did not call the police because you were getting your kicks watching someone being abused. ***SO NO, I FEEL NO REMORSE OR PITY FOR THE BLACK RACE GLOBALLY BECAUSE WE***

___INDULGE IN SLACKNESS AND NASTINESS.___ We don't think thus our ignorance and nasty ways is catching up to us, thus ___LOVEY HAVE AND HAS TRULY LEFT US TO LIVE OUR DISGUSTING AND MEANINGLESS LIVES.___

You cannot beat your women and children like that come on now. A woman gave birth to you for crying out loud.

What the fuck are you telling yourself and others; women, including your Mother and Lovey?

When you fucking beat a woman, are you not telling your Mother and Lovey that you do not give a fuck about females?

Lovey is both Male and Female. Lovey's choice for giving his message are females. His true chosen few are females not males. We carry his bloodline for lack of better words and not males. We are the ones to nurture and care, not you the male to the way you abuse and kill everything including good and true life.

If you treat a **_good woman_** right and with respect ___THERE IS ABSOLUTELY NO WAY IN HELL THAT GOOD WOMAN WOULD CHEAT ON YOU OR SIDE WITH ANYONE AGAINST YOU BECAUSE SHE KNOWS THE GOODNESS IN YOU.___ Some of you men cheat den guh home and beat unnu woman fi unnu infidelity. Some a unnu c***suckers listen to people tell unnu fi disrespect and treat woman like they are second class citizens; have no worth. ***MORONS; WITHOUT WOMEN YOUR ASSES YOU WOULD NOT EXIST.*** Earth is female; she gives birth to life as well as maintain life. But to the way you treat her and females globally you would think otherwise. ***THUS SOME MEN ARE SHIT AND NOT WORTH THE TIME NOR DAY OF LIFE LITERALLY.***

We as black people (not all but some) are a disgrace and embarrassment to life. *People beheading children and sodomising little children in Jamaica, but yet unnu lash out pon gays and many a unnu batty fucking tun up wuse dan wen oman dey pon dem period to claate.* No wonder JamaicaF because you're all fucking hypocrites and parasites that have no loyalty to self, land, people and Lovey. So what you the black race now gets is truly deserving because Lovey's window and door was closed to the lots of you long. ***YOU CAUSED ZION TO FAIL AND YES HER IGNORANCE CAUSED ZION TO FAIL.***

YOU CAUSED THIS DESTRUCTION ON SELF. INSTEAD OF REDEEMING YOU, YOU SINNED MORE VILED THUS CONDEMNING SELF AND LAND TO HELL. SO ACCEPT YOUR DESTRUCTION AND TRUE DEFEAT BECAUSE IF I HAVE MY OWN WAY, I WOULD SAVE NONE OF YOU.

You cannot call yourself black people; the first creation and watch blacks globally go down to hell.

You cannot say you are true love and you love true and watch your truth die. You have to hold on to your truth.

No, I am not being an hypocrite and I would not tell you to fight a man that is abusing his wife and child. You don't know the intent of the person but you can call the police and let them intervene. I don't know you and I am not trying to be an hero. I see the fire and I would not run into a burning house to save me nor would I want you to do this for me. I cannot give up my life for you nor would I want you to give up your life for me but if you can call the police call the police. Something could have been done to aid the woman and child. ***And I truly don't see why when a man is telling a woman to let go of them, they have to be still holding onto the fucking man.*** *Di man a fuck lick yu, let him the fuck go. Paane a BC rock stone and gi im one fuck lick. Do not lick im fi kill im, but fucking defend yourself.* Some of these BC man only ha mouth fi oman and nothing else. Defend you. *NO, I DO NOT CONDONE VIOLENCE BUT MY SPIRIT IS LIVID RIGHT NOW. And yes I was wrong to suggest violence because this is usually not me. I am a non violent person and I see how violence can erupt.* ***INJUSTICE STIRS THE SPIRIT TO ANGER; VIOLENCE.*** So whatever you do, ***do not listen to me on the violence front because I am truly wrong. I loathe certain injustice especially abuse; the abuse of women.*** No man has the right and no woman has the right to abuse another human being come on now. *You didn't fucking birth me; so don't fucking hit me.* Yes I know ***SOME OF US IT WAS DRILLED IN OUR HEADS NOT TO FIGHT. I WAS ONE OF THEM, BUT TO WHAT I WENT THROUGH IN MY LIFE, NO MAN CAN COME AND FUCKING ABUSE ME AGAIN.*** I refuse to allow it and I refuse to let anyone bully my children. Who the fuck are you for me to give up my right and rights to life to. Fuck you and chuck. Some of you are just service jockeys to service the urge and pleasures of some women. Your ass isn't needed ***(and I am going to get vile and nasty here people because my temper is boiling).*** You're just a fuck when some women need a fuck and nothing else. You're all pussy relievers and nothing else. After the fuck is done, who the fuck need some of you? And now a day's women don't need you, they have vibrators and all the sex toys they need at hand. It's only a matter of time before they make that human looking robot to satisfy a woman's every need if they haven't done so already. So chuck off to you the female and male abusers, the world don't need ya; you're all fucking waste matter. It's time for us women to wake up and truly love our self and let all abusive men and women including children go. ***Abuse in truly not needed because it breeds hate.*** Some people are bullied to the point where they commit suicide. Some children bully their parents. I have some that want to bully me but truss mi, when I move out and leave dem claate di door will be infinitely and indefinitely closed to them because dem don't cherish and or care about goodness. All they see is self, so I am going to let them fall on their own BC sword because they are not deserving of a good parent. No matter how you talk to them for their own good, they move and walk in the opposite direction.

Yes this is my sin and I repent not of it. Yes I know not all blacks are like this thus ***SOME ARE TRULY SAVED WHILE THE MAJORITY ARE NOT.***

Those blacks on the first level of Lovey's mountain has and have a saving grace but those at the top, truly good luck because you truly have none in me. Thus the first level of life was my choice. This level include the earth and the goodness of earth and her waterways; environment. I have to petition Lovey for the environment of earth because nature; the environment is truly good to life; thus the waterways of life here on earth and in the universe including the spiritual realm.

Ah yes the Jesus lie that man is banking on. Truly good luck with that because I know death and the demons of hell.

I know for a fact that DEATH WILL NOT LET ONE MAN SERVE YOUR SENTENCES.

The demons of hell have to get paid people. They have to play and your spirit is their game; play here on earth and in hell also. Demons do not take turns people. When it comes to you they want you, they want to have fun. So why would death allow you to go free *WHEN THEIR TRUE CHILDREN HAVE TO HAVE FUN; GET PAID?*

Why have one when death can have billions.
One serves no purpose to death come on now, but billions are a lot more fun and play.

Yes it's sad that the internet and or Social Media has and have become an outlet for sin.

It's unfortunate that you have to see such abuse in Jamaica and across the globe. There is truly no respect for life, ***thus when the dryness of the harvest come and you cannot find food and water, truly don't blame Lovey or anyone but self. LOVEY AND DEATH DID NOT CAUSE THIS, YOU DID.***

Wow because billions of you have your names on your containment unit in hell already. So truly good luck in getting a saving grace because once death owns you, sin and or death do all to keep you.

Michelle

Di head mash up; gone
Too much thinking
Too much care

I want to be void of all emotions
Want to be void of my caring and truthful nature
Ways

I want to be lost in me
Say fuck it
Fuck Lovey
Fuck the world
Fuck everything

In all I seek, I've found the lack of truth in a God; being that say He or She loves so.

Loving so is bullshit, thus Lovey is nothing but bullshit.

MAN HAS WILL YES; THUS MAN KILL TO GAIN IT ALL; CONTROL.

Thus the God and Lovey syndrome is bullshit; fucked because as ole people sey, nuh betta barrel nuh betta herring. So both death and life is the same thing to me on this day. We're all fucked either way.

Yes there is a God to say no, but what is saying no when he cannot keep you truly away from all evil.

What is the point of having a god that allows evil and depression to reach you? What is the point if you have to go into hell; face hell here on earth with him?

So life and God is bullshit because they are men; played out on the battlefield of man. Thus life and death is confusing for some but agony for those who know the truth. So why choose at all?

Why not leave life and death alone and say; Fuck you God, Fuck you Death, fuck everything because I choose nothing?

But then you're still fucked because nothing is something . So either way you still have to make a choice.

So yes life and death is fuckry because no one is truly free from the both of them.

Thus our spirit is trapped by the cranium; thus inhibiting our freedom to roam freely here on earth.

So yes, life and death are both bitch niggas because they inhibit you. Thus your true life is lost whilst decaying in the prison or grave of bones that surround us; infuse with our flesh.

Michelle
October 20, 2015

There are days when I truly don't want to think.
Days when I truly don't care what happens in this world to humans.

Days when I want to disassociate myself from the Lovey and or the God syndrome.

Days that I want to be free in my own little world of true freedom. My space that I can do what I want when I want and how I want. Who needs the confined space of this world; the environment we live in.

Our soul and spirit isn't free. It's trapped in its jail cell within our body. So how are we free and why can't our spirit and or soul escape the prison walls that surrounds it?

So humans are truly not free in this way. Yes this is a bummer but maybe one day, our spirit will find a way to freedom without the shedding of flesh.

Maybe the flesh and spirit will join as one and float from here to there in a conscious state.

Is this possible?

Of course it is, but knowing how to do this is the key. I don't know how to do this because if I did, I would truly not be here on earth. I would be gone quicker than you could say Jesus wept. I don't know, but I truly do not want a diverse world where I live with humans and or people that rape and rob; kill.

I truly do not want a diverse world where people create diseases to eradicate other human beings in the name of supremacy and or population control.

I truly do not want a diverse world where you are judged by your skin tone and sexuality, political and religious affiliations.

I truly don't need all this bullshit around me, hence I truly do not need a diverse world that incorporates sin and all the bullshit wicked and evil; envious and jealous people do.

This life that we live in is bullshit already. So why would I want or need another world filled with more bullshit; bullshit of lies and evil? Don't need it; thus I do not want a diverse world where people come and invade my naturally good and harmonious space.

Nope, don't want God or Lovey there either because the realm of God is bullshit if you can leave your children and people to starve; die despite us being given WILL.

It's bullshit when you are hungry and fed up of living and the God you say you look to cannot speak to you often. So yes, the realm of Lovey is bullshit and he knows it thus I tell you about it. Well in my way since this is my heart to heart with him and I truly don't care on this day. No people; there need to be an escape route for me but in truth, there isn't. So I need to rebel against all I know and live my life the way I want and need to. But when you are joined to Lovey you are restricted in travel and he keeps you poor financially. So all that you want to do, you cannot. So many do lose their way and join the other side and to be totally honest with you people, I truly do not blame them. Things aren't made easy for you, thus walking on the pathway of truth is truly not easy but extremely hard. Your life is not the same because you feel as if it's a joke; you're a joke. You are made an example of for the wicked to pounce on and destroy both physically and spiritually.

It's October 23, 2015 and yesterday the feeling was downcast and a bit insane. It's like you walk on the borderline of insanity sometimes. Thus your writing; well my writings can be dark and iffy at times. This is me and I truly want and need you to see this. Yes this is my heart to heart and I did not want to put dreams in this book because I want to break away from them but the dreams cannot be helped. I cannot live my life by my dream world and I truly don't. I try to show you what I see and I know for a fact that many will not like it, nor will they like what I say about them. I do not object to this; you not liking what is in these books. What I object to and will forever object to is you and or someone using Voodoo or Obeah against me. I do not stand for this fuckry thus I am fucking livid this morning. No I did not want to swear so much in this book despite it being my heart to heart, but when you have fucking demon duppies in the living and the spiritual world that is interfering with you then we fucking have a problem. ***You cannot hurt someone by muzzling them and taking their prosperity from them.***

You cannot muzzle someone by taking their life from them just because you don't like the fucking truth.

I was given the truth; information because Lovey told me to write a book and this is what I've been doing. *Now you want to end my life with your Obeah bullshit. Who the fuck do you think I am.* Pork is fucking nasty and by you setting your BC table with pork for me tells me of your nastiness and it will not work because as of this day, ***October 23, 2015, I CONDEMN EVERY SHAMAN, OBEAH MAN, WOMAN AND CHILD, EVERY VODOO PRIEST AND PRIESTESS, EVERY WITCH AND WARLOCK, EVERY ENCHANTER OF THE DEAD, EVERY DUPPY FEEDER, EVERY SCIENCE MAN AND WOMAN INCLUDING CHILDREN GLOBALLY AND IN THE SPIRITUAL REALM TO HELL MORE THAN INFINITELY AND INDEFINITELY FOR MORE THAN INFINITE AND INDEFINITE LIFETIMES AND GENERATIONS MORE THAN FOREVER EVER. In the name of Good God and Allelujah you are condemned, you are condemned, you are condemned.*** You do not hurt people with your nastiness of bullshit and evil. It matters not if you use people as sacrifice or how you pay death to kill, it matters not the lodge or order of death you belong. ***YOU ARE ALL CONDEMNED. EVERY EVIL THAT YOU DO TO OTHERS,***

<u>EVERY OBEAH, SCIENCE OR VOODOO, ENCANTATIONS THAT ALL OF YOU DO GLOBALLY, MUST TURN BACK ON YOU RIGHT NOW AS OF OCTOBER 23, 2015. YOUR NAMES INCLUDING NUMBER OF DEATH IN DEATH DUE TO YOUR EVILS MUST SEAL YOU INDEFINITELY IN THE JAIL CELLS OF HELL. Your children and family members that participate in this nastiness of sin must be condemned with you, thus they must go to hell with you. Thus saith the Lord thy God, meaning it is so.</u>

I am fed up, fed up of di Obeah bullshit. I see the shit that you are going to do before they happen and I am livid.

You do not take money to kill.
You do not take money to hurt others.

Your gift was meant for good not evil, but you see it befitting to hurt others for profit. So as of this day, October 23, 2015 Lovey let the evils of them that go to these people globally and universally to hurt others more than infinitely turn against them and their families.

Everything must be taken from these people and the Obeah, Voodoo, Science, Incantations of nastiness turn back on them. All the favour they seek from the dead and death must turn against them, the Obeah man, Obeah woman, Voodoo Priest, Priestess, Witch, Warlock, Chanter, Spellbinder and the person and or people who go to these people to hurt others and seek favours. Evil must be rendered powerless Lovey. None can use the earth, the universe, the spiritual realm, the dead for favour of the evil kind anymore. Let the dead that they seek favour from haunt anyone who seek favour from them when it comes to evil and wickedness.

No Lovey it's not fair. I am tired of these wicked people.

I am fed up as to why you would allow these people to hurt others including me. You asked me for something; a home and you are going to let nasty and wicked people continue to reach and hurt me; take my prosperity from me because of what is shown to me.

Why ask me to write then?

When these people hurt me, are they not hurting you also Lovey?

So why allow them to continually take me from you?

Why permit them to hinder me in all that I try to do for you and me including our good and true others? Is hindrance not hatred Lovey? So why do you do it, why do you and others hinder me? You cannot ask a person to write and then take their joy and truth; fun from them, come on now.

Thus you are not true and you can only love so. I refuse evil access to you but you cannot do the same when it comes to me. Return evil to sender Lovey. As I'm trying to build you, build me also. Let those that are going to go to these people (obeah and science people; the wicked agents of Satan and or the devil) to hurt me fail. Let them be the ones the obeah and or science and or voodoo fall back on. Take away from their prosperity. Let their family be the ones to have nothing come on now. You don't hurt someone that is not hurting you. ***YOU SEE THE COLOUR OF YOUR SINS; YOU KNOW WHAT THEY LOOK LIKE IN THE SPIRITUAL REALM. TRY TO DO ALL TO AMEND YOUR SINS AND OR WICKED WAYS HERE ON EARTH SO THAT YOU DO NOT END UP IN HELL COME ON NOW.***

I am not hurting you so why do you think I am a threat to you? Amend your stinking ways if you have stinky ways. This is what Lovey is trying to show you and tell you. YOU DON'T WANT TO GO TO HELL; SO WHY DO ALL THAT IS WICKED AND EVIL IN THE LIVING AND OR HERE ON EARTH TO GET THERE? SAVE YOU BECAUSE YOU CAN. YOU ARE ALIVE NOW, SO DO NOW AND NOT WAIT UNTIL LATER COME ON NOW. Life isn't about death it's about life. You have life here on earth so use your life wisely. Break away from evil because time is truly serious right now. Nations are taking in people from other nations as refugees thus they are taking up the responsibility and burdens of these people. They are taking from their own people spiritually and financially by taking on the burdens of another country. Like I said, I've seen the barren lands in Africa and if the East and West think that they are safe from the destruction that is coming; they had truly better think again.

Like I've said in another book, A MAN OR WOMAN INCLUDING CHILD THAT HAS NO PEACE CANNOT KEEP THE PEACE. THEIR HEARTS ARE NOT CLEAN AND NEVER WILL BE CLEAN BECAUSE THEY ARE TRULY NOT TRUE. THEY CREATE WARS FOR YOU TO FEEL SORRY FOR THEM AND WHEN THEY GET ACCESS TO YOUR LAND, THEY RAPE YOU OF EVERYTHING INCLUDING YOUR SPIRITUALITY.

SOME PEOPLE ARE SAYING IT'S THE GODLY THING TO DO. BUT I SAY UNTO YOU, IF A MAN OR WOMAN INCLUDING CHILD IS NOT OF GOD NOR ARE THEY LOOKED UPON BY LOVEY AND OR GOD, HOW CAN YOUR EFFORTS BE GODLY? HOW CAN WHAT YOU DO BE THE GODLY THING TO DO? YOUR EFFORTS ARE IN VAIN AND LOVEY WILL TURN AGAINST YOU BECAUSE YOU ARE ROBBING YOUR OWN TO FEED SOMEONE ELSE. YOU ARE TAKING THE FOOD OFF YOUR TABLE TO FEED DOGS; PEOPLE THAT ARE NOT DESERVING OF IT. PLUS YOU ARE GOING AGAINST LOVEY BECAUSE LOVEY DID NOT TELL YOU TO TAKE ON

THE NEXT MAN'S OR COUNTRY'S BURDEN. YOU ARE SINNING SELF AND LAND INCLUDING THE PEOPLE IN YOUR LAND.

EVIL CANNOT CHANGE NOR CAN EVIL BE REFORMED.

I TRULY DON'T KNOW WHY ANYONE THINK THEY CAN CHANGE AND OR CONVERT THE DEVIL.

EVIL AND OR THE DEVIL IS OF SIN AND NOTHING THAT YOU DO TO HELP SIN AND OR THE DEVIL'S PEOPLE IS LOOKED UPON AS GOOD BY LOVEY.

WHEN YOU BRING SIN IN YOUR HOME THEY DESTROY YOU AND THIS IS WHAT'S GOING TO HAPPEN TO A LOT OF SO CALLED WHITE NATIONS.

YOU KEEP AMALGAMATING SIN'S PEOPLE WITH YOUR PEOPLE WITHOUT KNOWING THAT WHEN YOU DO THIS, YOU ARE TAKING AWAY FROM THE PROSPERITY OF YOUR PEOPLE. YOU ARE GOING TO HAVE TO FEED, SHELTER, CLOTHE, PROVIDE MEDICAL CARE FOR THESE PEOPLE WHILST YOUR PEOPLE WHO ARE AT HOME THAT NEED THESE SERVICES CANNOT GET IT. SO TELL ME WHAT GOOD ARE YOU DOING FOR YOUR OWN WHEN YOU FEED OTHERS WITHOUT CARING FOR YOUR OWN? Do for your own before you can do for others come on now.

Why should Lovey Look upon you and cherish you and your land when you rob from your own to feed the devil's own? Thus no one will like me because I HAVE A SOUTHERN MENTALITY. THUS SEPARATION ALL THE WAY I SAY. DON'T WANT YOU IN MY LAND AND I TRULY DON'T CARE WHAT YOUR LAND DO TO YOU IF YOU ARE WICKED AND EVIL AND NOT OF LOVEY.

And don't try it with the converting bullshit because Lovey is true life and not death. You live for death so bleeping die with death. You serve no good purpose here on earth so why the hell should I give up my place with my Beloved for heathens like you? You are infinitely and indefinitely more than forever ever shut out of my world and kingdom because TRUE PEACE; NO FORM OF TRUTH AND GOODNESS IS IN YOUR HEARTS. IF YOU HAD TRUE PEACE AND LIVED FOR TRUTH AND CLEANLINESS YOUR LEADERS WOULD NOT CREATE WARS AND KILL YOU; FEED YOU CRAP AND BULLSHIT OF HATRED WHEN IT COMES TO OTHER NATIONS.

IF YOUR LEADERS WERE TRULY PEACEFUL, THEY WOULD NOT CREATE STRIFE AND HATRED AMONGST YOU IN YOUR LAND FOR OTHERS TO FEEL SORRY FOR YOU SO THAT YOU CAN GAIN ACCESS INTO THE LAND OF OTHERS TO CONTAMINATE AND DESTROY THE PEOPLE.

LIFE IS NOT DEATH AND IF YOU HAD TRULY WANTED PEACE; GOODNESS, THE GOODNESS OF LOVEY, YOU

WOULD BE LIVING YOUR LIFE GOOD AND CLEAN AND PUT DOWN THE FIGHTING AND WAR BULLSHIT.

<u>YOU ARE MURDERERS.</u> THUS ISLAM WAS POLLUTED AND CONDEMNED BY THE LOTS OF YOU AND LOVEY; ALLELUJAH; ALLAH TO YOU; LOCKED YOUR LYING AND DECEIVING ASSES OUT OF HIS KINGDOM INDEFINITELY MORE THAN FOREVER EVER. HUMANITY FORGOT THAT IN THEIR BOOK OF SIN AND EVIL; MAN'S SO CALLED HOLY BIBLE, ENMITY AND STRIFE WAS PUT BETWEEN GOOD AND EVIL. <u>LOVEY DID NOT PUT THIS ENMITY AND STRIFE THERE; EVIL DID.</u> EVIL DO NOT LIKE ANYONE THAT IS GOOD AND TRUE THUS EVIL DO ALL TO FIGHT AND KILL GOODNESS. THUS THE STRIFE; HATRED THAT WAS PUT INTO PLAY FROM THE GET GO. SO I TRULY DON'T CARE ABOUT DEATH'S CHILDREN BECAUSE THEY ARE TRULY NOT ONE OF US. THEY LIVE TO KILL THUS THE KILLING SPREES THAT THEY DO HERE ON EARTH.

<u>TRUTH CANNOT KILL NOR CAN TRUTH DIE. LIES AND SIN DIES BUT TRUTH CANNOT DIE. TRUTH IS LIFE EVERLASTING AND HUMANITY FAIL TO SEE THIS.</u>

I truly do not comprehend why anyone would think that Lovey would protect and save the devil's own. If you are not of Lovey I will not save you.

*Besides I cannot give to the devil or take from the devil. Death will not permit you taking from them; so I truly don't know why humans would think otherwise. <u>THE SEAL OF DEATH NO ONE CAN BREAK IF THEY ARE NOT ORDAINED TO. DEATH DO NOT PERMIT ANYONE TAKING FROM THEM</u> THUS YOU WERE TOLD, <u>**"THE WAGES OF SIN IS DEATH AND TRUTH IS LIFE EVERLASTING."**</u> So if you do not have the truth and if you do not live by the truth, you cannot live, you must die. No one can change this law. If you are of Lovey, you do not want to change this law nor do you want to save the wicked and evil of this world and universe including the spiritual realm.*

GOOD AND EVIL DO NOT BELONG TOGETHER. THEY CANNOT COEXIST IN PEACE AND I TRULY DO NOT COMPREHEND WHY PEOPLE WOULD THINK OTHERWISE. WE HAVE FREE WILL; THE WILL TO CHOOSE HERE ON EARTH AND MANY (BILLIONS) OF YOU DID NOT CHOOSE LIFE. YOU CHOSE DEATH SO DEATH MUST TAKE YOU. THE 24000 YEARS MAN GOT TO DECEIVE IS UP THUS DEATH COMES. We were to choose good over evil in that 24000 year period and billions did not choose good; they chose evil and I told you this above, so truly good luck to billions of you. The devil and his children knew the time of evil has come to an end thus they seek asylum in other lands so that they can continue on with their lies and deceit. And like I've told Lovey, I want and need no Babylonian in our land. I will not save anyone that is wicked and evil. I refuse to; so truly do not give them access to the land that I go into and call my home. Keep the devil and their children at bay and the hell away and far from me. I truly do not want to see what happens to them because I WILL NOT SHARE ANY OF THE GOODNESS HE LOVEY HAS AND HAVE GIVEN TO ME WITH THEM. What he Lovey has and have given me must share with our good and true people. Anyone that say let's share with them (the devil's people) will be immediately evicted into the devil's kingdom. You see and know the lies and evils; deceit of these people and you are going to have compassion for them. When they were enslaving your ancestors' ass, raping them, murdering them, stealing their wealth and prosperity, keeping them and us from Lovey, did they have compassion? No they did not. So why the bleep should I have compassion for any of them? Our beloved was taken from us. Many of our ancestors' children were killed without mercy and you want me to have compassion for the devil's own? Hell no. Thus the heart has no true love for them because they are truly wicked and evil. I NEED TRUE PEACE AND I WILL NOT SACRIFICE MY BELOVED AND PEOPLE; TRUE FAMILY FOR THEM. I REFUSE TO COME ON NOW.

ONWARDS I GO

I see your bullshit before it happens thus I am pissed.

Everyone has a right to live but for some of you they don't. This is why some of you kill, create diseases to kill, pay others to kill. ***THIS IS SAD BECAUSE MANY OF YOU THAT DO THIS; DECEIVE PEOPLE AND KILL, DON'T REALIZE THAT THE SINS OF YOUR DECEIVED FALL BACK ON YOU.***

ALL WHO YOU INLIST OR ENLIST TO KILL; THEIR SINS FALL ON YOUR TABLE. BECAUSE OF DECEIT LOVEY CAN SAY, YOU PERSON XY DECEIVED PERSON XX AND OR YOU PERSON XX DECEIVED PERSON XY AND BECAUSE OF THIS DECEIT, I AM GOING TO FORGIVE PERSON XX OR XY AND YOU THE DECEIVED MUST TAKE ON THEIR SINS. I AM TRANSFERRING THEIR SINS TO YOU AND THERE ISN'T A DAMNED THING DEATH CAN DO ABOUT IT. YOU LIED, THUS I AM GIVING PERSON XX AND OR XY ACCESS TO MY

KINGDOM AND NOT YOU. This can happen thus I tell you, do not give up trying. Deceit is a bitch and if you are deceived, you have hope. Hope is given on this day because Lovey does remember you. Walk in your glory because it's not right for someone to take your life and right from you.

And you Lovey, I want to blast you but will refrain from my anger in this book because I did unleash my fury on you earlier this morning. How the hell can you tell me; you know what let me forget it and wane my temper with you BECAUSE YOU ARE TRULY NOT LOYAL IN MY BOOK ON THIS DAY. Yes you are showing me the table that's been set for me but really Lovey?

Fam and people, my BC own more than fucking nasty.

Di fuckry of Obeah and Voodoo haffi stop now man come on now. I truly have to wane my temper because like I said, in another book in the Michelle's Jean Book Series; if mi opin mi mouth Jamaica mash up to di bullshit some of these artists do to get success.

Dem fucking nasty and for you the Rasta community that's going to set me up. <u>Listen to di Razz Attack Medley AN HEAR WEY DEMARCO TELL DI TRAITOR DEM. CONSIDER YOURSELF TOLD.</u>

Unnu chat bout unnu real an unnu bless; guh fuck unnuself because unnu join forces with the original traitors DAT SELL OUT GOD; LOVEY. None a unnu can chat to mi because NUFF A UNNU SPRINKLE POWDA LIKE BATH WATER AND WUK OBEAH WUSE DAN DI PEOPLE DEM INNA AFRICA AND DI CARIBBEAN COMBINED.

Unnu fucking wutless because LODGE MAN AND OMAN NOA UNNU CLAATE. UNNU NUH CLEAN DAS WHY UNNU JOIN FORCES WITH DEATH AND CARRY DEATH EVERY WHERE UNNU GUH. LOOK PAN UNNU BLOODCLAATE HEAD. FUCK UNNU WITH UNNU BC OBEAH. Das why Jamaica and black people caane betta. An yes to di nassi oman inna mi dream I went there. Du something nuh if yu can. Nuff a unnu a fucking leggo beast because unnu sit pan road kawna anna beg fi fucking what lef an caane pay unnu fucking rent. Das why Jamaica is in so much fucking debt and disarray all around. Bunch of fucking scam artist.

Some a unnu dey inna people ouse an caane pay fi unnu rent; an wen lanlaade cum fi tek unnu outta dem place, dem caane get unnu out because unnu set unnu self inna dem place suh dem caane get unnu out.

There's a price to pay for your sins and that time is coming thus unnu nuh waane pay unnu rent; dues. Thus Jamaica has a National Debt Load of $20 Billion US. A debt load that Jamaica cannot repay, thus Jamaicans are locked the fuck in hell and it's only a fucking matter of time before hell is unleashed on the lots of you right here on earth.

Unnu noh noa fucking pain because your drought has been fucking ordained by a higher force that you don't know about. Cleanliness is not with any of you, thus Lovey put in the sky; *JamaicaF and told me Jamaica is unclean. Unnu naah live pon borrowed time, unnu a live pon dead time; THE TIME OF DEATH* and it's a matter of time before your time (666) reach your hypocritical asses.

So yes you are truly the Sodomites and Gomorrahites of old and today. YOU CANNOT BE SAVED BECAUSE LOVEY REFUSE ME ACCESS TO YOUR LAND. I AM FORBIDDEN TO SAVE THE LOTS OF YOU. UNNU TOO FUCKING WICKED.

Fuck unnu an unnu Obeah because unnu obeah a wha a condemn island and people right now.

Thus people (artist) like Razz Attack, Demarco, Stephen Marley, Buju Banton, Konshens, Bob Marley and others tell the world about the lots of you including them.

Cleanliness does not live or lie in any of you because UNNU A DUPPY. THUS UNNU WALK AND LIVE LIKE THE BC DEAD IN THE LIVING.

Thus my dream with the white man; demon white man that came to me in his BC Rasta colours in his eye. Never have I seen anyone with these colours in their eye and surrounding them before. No he was not dressed in the Rasta colours; he had the colours in his eye and surrounding him like I said. Before I saw this man, I went into this restaurant (eatery) and went to this table, you know what let me leave this dream alone because I know about pork and how people use pork inna obeah. Therefore, di pig is the filthiest animal in the spiritual realm. Thus the nastiness some of my own black people indulge in to keep their own down as well as kill dem. To the Rasta community, *I see you and nastiness unnu a pree for me thus your condemnations will come back to haunt the lots of you. FI UNNU GOD ANNO BLACK. FI UNNU GOD A WHITE BECAUSE IT'S A WHITE GOD; THE GOD OF DEATH ALL OF YOU SERVE; THIS I TRULY KNOW NOW. THUS THIS DREAM AND THE DREAM I HAD LONG AGO WITH PETER TOSH CONFIRMS THIS; THUS THE TRUTH OF ALL OF YOU.*

No Rasta serves Lovey because none of you are of him. THUS THE BLACK ANGELS BOTH MALE AND FEMALE HAVE DREDS; DREADLOCKS. Yes some has long flowing braids but true death comes in the form of Rastas and this NO ONE CAN CHANGE BECAUSE IT'S THE FULL TRUTH; THUS SAITH THE LORD THY GOD MEANING IT IS SO.

Unnu mek di global community think unnu, clean but cleanliness far from the lots of you. So no matter the obeah wey a fling; know that death keep the secret for no man, and it's death you are all going to see.

Death is waiting for the lots of you because no one that is evil can escape death. SINS BRING ABOUT DEATH; THUS MANY LANDS AND PEOPLE ARE DYING RIGHT NOW. SO I WORRY NOT ABOUT THE FUCKING LOTS OF YOU AND WHAT YOU WANT TO DO. THERE'S AN APP FOR THE LOTS OF YOU, AND THAT APP IS MFING HELL.

DEATH DID NOT CREATE DEATH. HUMANS GAVE BIRTH TO DEATH WITH THEIR SINS. SO TRULY GOOD LUCK TO THE LOTS OF YOU WITH YOUR OBEAH CRAP AND SHIT.

Opportunity is not found in Jamaica, nor is prosperity. Thus every time I try with the lots of you my prosperity is taken from me. Thus this morning the huge green food that had the colour of watermelons on this tree. The tree full a green food. I can't remember if a nutmeg mi si pon di tree, but the food huge and long. Some were in the shape of zucchini and squash; the long yellow ones. But like I said, in the dream; they had the colour of watermelons. Hence the huge disappointments that are coming in my life yet again when it comes to my own black people. But you know what; I cannot be bothered because you have to have more than strength and will power to deal with my own black people. It's not an easy road with them; thus

Lovey knows this first hand to some of the crap and shit some of us as black people do.

Eeee come eene like wi destined fi failure and ignorance.

Dean Loyal said it best in his song Print Pon Dem Face.

AND NO, I TRULY AND CATEGORICALLY DO NOT ENDORSE THIS ARTIST DUE TO HIM DEVIL AN WURL BOSS FUCKRY WEY IM PROMOTE.

Thus Jamaica cannot be better economically and spiritually. Wi tek up di fuckry of other nations and destroy our own and when yu try show dem dis, dem sey a lie yu a tell. Im affi endorse di bible and the Kartel fuckry thus many bleach dem skin without knowing that when you bleach your skin you are accepting spiritual death in the living. You have handed your life (earthly and spiritual life) over to the devil thus giving up all chances to be saved in the end.

Yes my dream world is jacked up and many black men in my dream world is hell bound fi real. No people, I saw flowers, these beautiful flowers. This young black male was cultivating them; he had a garden, no not a garden garden but he had planted flowers and he gave this guy beside me that seemed like my baby faada a flower. I could not see the guy's face that was beside me, but know that someone; a black male was beside me and we were partners I guess from the dream. The young male had planted flowers and they were beautiful of white and pink with a little black in them. I am lazy thus I won't Google search the flowers I am talking about. He the young black guy gave my partner a tree (stalk) but the tree (Stalk) broke into two pieces. ***With me being me now. I asked the young black male what is good for diabetes an di buoy tell mi Sinclebible (Aloe Vera) an bleach.*** People, yu si why mi nuh truss man especially black males in my dream world. Sinclebible an bleach. Dat a death in the living. Di buoy a gi mi death. So no, black people fucked in both worlds wen eee cum to fiwi owna lying and deceiving own. Thus it was after im tell mi dis mi si di tree with the oleheap a green food.

Yes disappointment, disappointment at the hands of my own thus the tree was full.

And if I am reading this dream that is for me wrong people truly let me know.

Am I tried?

I am truly tired thus the woman of Zion lost; fell and ran out of time in the spiritual realm. The fall of black people is there, so truly good luck to the lots of us globally.

• • •

Yes I get down on Lovey because I am truly tired of being the scapegoat for death; wicked and evil people.

I am truly tired of seeing my own black people selling themselves for a likkle piece a bread.

Hundreds of millions if not billions have and has condemned self and family to hell already without knowing.

FROM YOU TATTOO YOURSELF, YOU HAVE JOINED THE LEAGUE OF DEATH AND YOU HAVE TO SELL DEATH. YOUR SOUL IS NOT YOURS ANYMORE.

You've sold your soul to the devil and any child or children you have belong to death; the devil. So because of this, you must go to hell and burn. YOU CANNOT ESCAPE HELL BECAUSE YOU GAVE YOUR SOUL AND OR SPIRIT OVER TO DEATH IN THE LIVING.

Yes I said those who are deceived have and has hope. *But IT'S NOT ALL THAT WERE DECEIVED. MANY WILLINGLY GAVE UP THEIR SOUL FOR POWER, MONEY AND FAME. THESE PEOPLE HAVE NO HOPE BECAUSE THEY WILLINGLY SIGNED A CONTRACT WITH DEATH. Some listen to di Wurl Boss an bleach dem skin without knowing that di Wurl Boss gave up his soul to the devil fi fame and fortune; money. You the skin bleachers that followed him were his sacrifice unto death; thus the lots of you that follow him and endorse him have and has lost your soul literally. You have no chance in hell to be redeemed. You're all going to join him in hell; thus saith the Lord thy God meaning it is so.*

Some of you bleach your skin to look white due to self hate and money. **NOT ONE OF YOU REALIZE THAT WHEN YOU BLEACH YOUR SKIN IN THE LIVING, YOU ARE DENOUNCING YOUR BLACK FOUNDATION.**

WHEN YOU DO THIS (BLEACH YOUR SKIN), YOU ARE TELLING LOVEY YOU ARE NOT APART OF HIS FOUNDATION OF LIFE. YOU'VE ACCEPTED SPIRITUAL DEATH IN THE LIVING AND DEATH IS YOUR GOD; CHOICE.

WHEN YOU DO THIS, YOU CANNOT UNDER ANY CIRCUMSTANCES BE SAVED BECAUSE YOU ACCEPTED DEATH.

SO BECAUSE OF THIS ACCEPTANCE OF DEATH, YOU ARE GIVEN YOUR DOWNWARD TRIANGLE IN THE LIVING AND IN DEATH AND OR ONCE YOUR SPIRIT SHEDS THE FLESH. *And yes this is why some Rastas point their triangle down because they know they are of death and not of life. They made the choice of death so they follow death in the living.*

Thus Marcus Mosiah Garvey told us, "a people without knowledge of their history are like trees without roots," meaning they are dead.

Your choice is death in the living thus your family and or children must go to hell with you.

No one knows that death can be a bitch nigger and take your mother and father and other family members to hell with you because of you. So if you had a saving grace in the living, you no longer have one from the day you began to bleach your skin. You've disassociated yourself from life and accepted hell as your home.

You've forgotten that when they do this; accept death in the living, you have to face the severity of hell's fire. This willful contract Satan will not release you from. ***WHEN YOU SIGN A CONTRACT WITH DEATH, IT IS DEATH FOR DEATH. THIS CONTRACT IS BINDING IN AND OR ON EARTH AS WELL AS IN DEATH; THE SPIRITUAL REALM.***

ABSOLUTELY NO ONE CAN RELEASE YOU FROM THIS CONTRACT BECAUSE IT IS THAT BINDING; THUS IT IS SEALED. YOU HAVE THE MARK AND SEAL OF DEATH THUS YOU ARE KNOWN IN BOTH WORLDS. YOU'VE BECOME CAIN AND YOU MUST KILL FOR DEATH. *Genesis*

If you have a wife and child and or children, they belong to death also. You sealed their faith in hell with you. I keep telling you over and over again that, *"IT'S THE ONES THAT SAY THEY LOVE YOU THAT SCREW YOU UP AND TAKE YOUR LIFE FROM YOU."* They bring you to hell with them to die; thus love is hate and cannot be true. Love is evil and will never be good because love gives you over to death as a sacrifice to die.

Over the course of my life and in my dream world, I've come to realize that *BLACK PEOPLE ARE NOT LOYAL TO LIFE; TRUTH, NOR CAN THEY BE LOYAL TO LOVEY.* Every messenger Lovey has and have sent to the black race have and has faced hell with our people based on hue. Babylonians excluded. *NO ONE HAS SUCCEEDED IN SAVING US AS A RACE AND PEOPLE; NOT EVEN MOSES. HENCE MOSES TOOK THE YING AND YANG ALL THE WAY TO ASIA FOR SAFE KEEPING.*

We as a people have not figured it out yet.

We cannot figure it out because we truly do not want to. We want to belong so we integrate ourselves into societies that do not belong to us; societies we are not to go into.

Ask a black man about his true language he or she cannot tell you. They give you Arabic, Swahili, French, Portuguese and some other far out and whacked out language without knowing that our ancestors did not speak any of these languages. *THE LANGUAGE OF LOVEY CANNOT BE SPOKEN; IT CAN ONLY BE WRITTEN, AND IT'S ONLY A SELECTED FEW THAT CAN WRITE THIS LANGUAGE.*

We've forgotten about vibration and how vibration is a language not a wave length that man tell you about. This is the language of the spirit; ***thus humanity tells you BLACK PEOPLE EXCLUDING BABYLONIANS HAVE VIBE.*** We vibrate thus communicating with the spirit and or from spirit to spirit. This I've told you in some of my other books. Thus I do not want or need to belong in the devil's society of wickedness and Lovey knows this. Thus he's not truly loyal to goodness and truth; cleanliness and honesty in my book and yes on this day.

You cannot say you love so and show me the magnitude of loving so and not protect your good up good up own.

When these people initiate the obeah thought and sequence; they are not just going after me and my life, they are going after Lovey and his life. They are truly taking away goodness and truth from Lovey and Lovey knows this, but yet keep these scumbags of nastiness around. Why say you love so if you can't truly protect your true and unconditional own from the cesspool and cesspools of sin? Wicked and evil people that call themselves obeah man and woman, voodoo priests and priestesses, witches and warlocks, shamans and what have you.

Why the hell should these people continue to hurt others and plague this earth with their nastiness come on now?

Death and their people have no true right here on earth with your people Lovey, so why are you giving these people access to your good and true own?

Don't say one thing and do the opposite. You are not human come on now.

It's time to settle the score because I've told you, your temper is not as dangerous as mine. I have the bigger temper and it's time the foolishness of evil stop in my world. You hinder Lovey. You are the one hindering me from giving you your needs; especially your mega mansion.

Life, good and true life isn't about death Lovey but obviously you cannot see this.

Why the hell should I walk on the road of death with my own black people?

Look at the hell my grandmother went through and the same faith is befalling me.

Why the hell should this be? I've told you, you are rejected so step the bleep up and truly love you man come on now.

The fucking black race have and has sold you out. We are the ones to believe in all the shit they tell us without coming to you directly. BOB TOLD US THIS BUT WE REFUSE TO LISTEN. Despite his failures Lovey, we as a nation and people including him caused him to fail in truly educating us. I will not blame all on the people. I have to blame him too because he did things he was not supposed to do. He walked in the realm and on the pathway of death; so death had to take him before his time come on now. His resting place in not like the resting place of man even I know this. *When you are chosen you do not go to the same paradise as ordinary people.* You are separated and or put in a different world because your hell and or home (paradise) is not indefinite. Well your hell is not indefinite because you have a saving grace somehow. And Lovey if I've explained this wrong; truly forgive me and let me correct the mistakes I've made.

So as humans, we are the ones to give birth and rise to death because we were told the wages of sin is death. And some people Lovey, truly did not choose you, so you have to let them go in true peace.

Let the devil have their people.

I feel better now.

Just had a shower and was thinking about my dream with the young black male and his flowers and what he told me in regards to diabetes.

H2O2 (Hydrogen Peroxide) Food Grade. I was looking into this earlier and you can ingest H2O2 35% Food Grade in small drops. But you have to use the drops with distilled and or purified water. Not tap water due to the tap water mineral and or chemical content. Maybe this was what he was trying to tell me. Maybe I can add Sinclebible (Aloe Vera) to this and it will help me with my diabetes. But then I am still skeptical when it comes to this. I will search the health food stores for 35% or 12% food grade $H2O2$ and be a guinea hen not pig and see if this does in fact help my diabetes. Dear God I hope it does not kill me because I am not sure if you can add anything to the consumption of $H2O2$ whilst oxygenating my body. And yes for those of you that do not know, Hydrogen Peroxide is used as bleach in some salon products (hair products). Damn I need to be brave when it comes to this. I am scared shitless to try this.

Am I scared if someone formulates this and makes billions?

Hell no, as long as it works; truly help people that have uncontrollable diabetes. ***AND LET ME CLEAR THIS UP, THE YOUNG MAN DID NOT SAY SINCLEBIBLE AND BLEACH IS A CURE. HE SAID IT WOULD HELP.***

Yes some people will come and say they have the cure for diabetes. If it cures you hurray because you are blessed. Sinclebible is a healing source for certain ailments but you have to know how to take it. I will not say sinclebible and bleach cures because I was not told that it did. Like I said, bleach cannot be consumed because it's bleach. The only bleaching agent that can be consumed is food grade hydrogen peroxide and I truly do not know if this is the bleach that the young man meant. ***And as I said, I am leery and weary of males in the spiritual realm because nuff a dem lie.*** Thus we as humans are lied to in the physical realm. Men seek control and they do seek to kill; thus you have religion and politics that rob you of your soul and spirit; life here in the physical realm. I do not seek to control, nor do I seek dominance because *NONE OF US CAN TAKE THE BULLSHIT OF DOMINANCE AND CONTROL TO THE SPIRITUAL REALM. THUS HUNDREDS OF MILLIONS IF NOT BILLIONS ARE BURNING LIKE A BITCH IN HELL RIGHT NOW.*

NO ONE CAN DOMINATE AND CONTROL LIFE; NOR CAN ANYONE DOMINATE AND CONTROL DEATH. Life, good and true life is given; we are the ones as humans to turn our life into death with our sins.

Are the Pharmaceutical companies gonna want to X me out for this?

I would not be surprised because if this work; it will take away from their trillion dollar per year empire. See what I find is that, ***human life is not valued. YOU AND I COME DOWN TO AND OR BOIL DOWN TO THE DOLLAR BILL FOR SOME. The preservation of life is not the concern for those that control the FOOD CHAIN DISTRIBUTION. AS LONG AS YOU CONSUME AND INGEST THE CRAP YOU ARE BEING FED; THEN SOCIETY IS GOOD TO GO.*** Your health concerns no one because if you don't go to the doctor there would be no need for doctors and they would not get paid. Without the doctors prescribing these different medications; the pharmaceutical companies would go out of business because there would be no one to buy their crapping and slow killing drugs that kill you over time.

Without the pharmaceutical companies, chemical manufacturers would go out of business; certain farmers would not be needed and more importantly, governments would lose out on taxes all around, thus many in the public and or government sector would not have jobs.

So everything in life plays a role thus impacting you negatively and or positively. And yes, all of this affects the environment and resources of the earth.

With global warming that man created, we as humans are losing LAND SPACE. THE EARTH IS MOVING TOWARDS ITS WATER AGE AND YOU WILL FIND THE MASSIVE DESTRUCTION OF LANDS. SOME LANDS ARE GOING TO SINK AND MANY ARE GOING TO DIE OF STARVATION AND INADEQUATE DRINKING WATER.

The earth will not yield as much; thus the extinction of man; humans is inevitable.

So if the diseases that man creates in laboratories don't get you; then starvation will eventually get you; kill you.

• • •

As human beings we truly do not conserve. We waste including me; so truly think because like I've said, the life you save might just be your own.

We impact each other whether negatively or positively and the latter; negative must die. The time of Satan is up thus the gathering must begin. If you are not included in the over one hundred million that is slated to live; then truly good luck to you because you will not be saved despite hope; the hope given on this day and before.

Hundreds of millions if not billions of black people will truly not be saved and I've told you this above and in some of my other books. ***THE DEVIL AND OR SATAN IS BANKING ON THE BLACK RACE TO BRING DOWN LOVEY. HE SATAN DID WIN ON THE LOYALTY LEVEL WHEN IT COMES TO BLACK PEOPLE AND OR THE BLACK RACE. BABYLONIANS EXCLUDED BECAUSE YOU ARE NOT BLACK; ONE OF US.***

No one in the black community can say otherwise because all I have to do is point to the devil's mark and or brand; tattoos you've inked on your bodies to become a part of the devil's own. You have the mark of the beast because 666 and or triple six represent the time Satan, no, not Satan but his 3 daughters had to deceive humanity. Some of you say son but I saw them in the spiritual realm as females; these beautiful half caste and or biracial girls. Each had 6 in their forehead and I've told you this in some of my other books.

The devil had time, thus Satan's children had 18000 years to deceive humanity.

Satan had 6, six thousand years to rule; thus the time of death and or Satan is not 666 but 6666 which is 24000 years. I've told you this as well in some of my other books. ***ARMY TIME IS A REMINDER TO ALL THAT SATAN HAS 24000 YEARS TO DECEIVE HUMANITY THUS THE GOD OF WAR ARIES. And yes this is why war is global. IN ORDER TO GO TO HELL YOU HAVE TO DIE. YOU CANNOT LIVE AND YOU ALL KNOW THIS. WELL IF YOU DON'T NOW YOU KNOW.***

THE MORE A LEADER KILLS, SEND HIS PEOPLE TO WAR THE MORE INDEBTED YOUR COUNTRY GETS. THUS THE WAGES OF SIN IS DEATH AND I'VE TOLD YOU THIS BEFORE IN ANOTHER BOOK. NOT USING THE SAME WORDS BUT YOU GET THE GIST.

I've told you certain people you are not to marry nor can you marry. When you marry them yu life blighted. ***Some people do not recover and for some it takes years to get back on their feet again.*** *THIS IS THE SAME FOR SOME PEOPLE THAT YOU LET INTO YOUR LAND AND HOME. SOME PEOPLE YOU ARE NOT TO HAVE IN YOUR LAND OR HOME BECAUSE THEY BRING DESTRUCTION WITH THEM. THEY BLIGHT THE LAND AND HOME YOU ARE IN INCLUDING YOUR LIFE.* *SO TRULY BE CAREFUL ON WHO YOU LET INTO YOUR LAND AND HOME BECAUSE IT'S NOT*

EVERYONE THAT IS OF GOD; LOVEY AND WE ALL KNOW THIS. SOME PEOPLE ARE OF THE OTHER GOD AND THAT GOD IS DEATH.

A man or woman including child cannot kill and think that it will not affect the people in his country and or the land he or she lives in.

<u>ONE DEATH THAT IS WILLFULLY DONE DOES IMPACT ALL IN YOUR LAND INCLUDING THE LAND ITSELF.</u>

When you send your people on the battlefield to kill, you are taking away life from the people of your land as well as the land itself.

When this happens; death can claim all in your land and there isn't a damn thing you as a citizen can do about it. You were the ones to elect warmongers to oversee you.

A good politician do not put you the people and land in debt with death come on now.

A good leader do all to avoid war thus securing your life with Lovey, Good God and Allelujah all around. You all know this, but instead of doing right for you and country you do the latter; wrong.

I'VE TOLD YOU TIME AND TIME AGAIN IN SOME OF MY OTHER BOOKS THAT TRUTH CANNOT LIE AND DESPITE

WHAT I WRITE, DO YOUR BEST TO SEEK FAVOUR WITH LOVEY. SOME OF YOU TRULY DO NOT KNOW THE TRUTH AND THE TRUTH IS YOUR TRUE FREEDOM.

YOU WERE TOLD TRUTH IS EVERLASTING LIFE AND THIS CANNOT CHANGE BECAUSE TRUTH CANNOT LIE.

DEATH DOES NOT LIE TO YOU IN MANY WAYS. DEATH HAS A JOB TO DO BASED ON YOUR LIES; SIN THAT YOU DO HERE ON EARTH. THUS WE AS HUMANS GAVE BIRTH TO DEATH AND I DID TELL YOU THIS ABOVE.

<u>No one can run from life and death period.</u> One was given and the other you chose; gave birth to. THUS THE WILL OF MAN IS TRULY NOT CLEAN. IT IS DIRTY BECAUSE WE DO CHOOSE UNCLEAN THINGS HERE ON EARTH AND WE DO DO THEM. Thus I saw Will in the form of Will Smith.

<u>Therefore, the first man to be created WAS NOT NAMED ADAM, HE WAS NAMED WILL. THUS THE WILL OF MAN AS WE KNOW IT TODAY AND THIS I AM NOW FINDING OUT.</u>

Yes I told you about Will in another book and now I am over standing the full truth. See this is the thing with dreams. You have to figure them out and some are hard to figure out. So as we are told Adam was the first human, you now know that THIS INFORMATION AS GIVEN BY

YOUR SO CALLED HOLY BIBLE IS FALSE. If you read your so called holy bible correctly, you are given two creations. No, not two creation but one creation and one forming. Because it said, ***God formed man from the dust of the earth. THIS IS SIMPLY TELLING YOU THAT AS HUMAN BEINGS WE ARE PHYSICAL AND SPIRITUAL BEINGS. THE FLESH BEING PHYSICAL AND YOUR SOUL AND OR SPIRIT BEING SPIRITUAL.***

Once the spirit sheds the flesh, this is where the judgment of man and or life; true life come in depending on the type of life you live here on earth. And no, I am not contradicting myself due to wording. I have no better way to put it.

If you are a person of sin; meaning you have more sins on your life and death record then YOUR TRIANGLE GOES DOWN. YOU ARE GIVEN THE DOWNWARD TRIANGLE.

IF YOUR LIFE HERE ON EARTH IS GOOD, THEN YOU RECEIVE THE UPRIGHT TRIANGLE.

To take it further, you now know why some Rasta's point their triangle down. *THEY ARE FROM THE ORDER OF DEATH SO THEY SHOW YOU THIS BY POINTING THE TRIANGLE DOWN.* Thus I've told you; Rasta's keep the order of death. *THEY CANNOT KEEP THE ORDER OF LIFE*

BECAUSE THEY POINT THEIR LIFE DOWNWARD. Therefore, death owns them. Yes they will tell you otherwise but this is the truth. I'VE TOLD YOU TIME AND TIME AGAIN THAT SATAN LOVES BLACK PEOPLE; THE BLACK RACE. HE PLAYS THEM TO THE POINT WHERE "HELL IS FULL OF BLACK PEOPLE AND RECRUITING MORE."

Give the black race lies and they run with it whilst claiming it's the truth when it's not the truth. THIS IS ALSO WHY MOSES COULD NOT LEAVE TRUTH; LIFE WITH US. WE ARE NOT A LOYAL SET OF PEOPLE. MOSES HAD TO TAKE LIFE OUT OF EGYPT AND BRING IT INTO ASIA FOR SAFE KEEPING. Yes Asians are a part of the black race but they've disassociated themselves from us. If you look at history; our history you cannot blame them. So now, due to the falling of Zion, Asians must now take the place of her; the Black Woman of Zion. They are more powerful and they know the truth thus the Ying and Yang.

As blacks we take up cultures and shit that do not belong to us and say it is ours. Thus Marcus Mosiah Garvey told us, "a people without knowledge of their history are like trees without roots," meaning we are dead. And we are dead because Revelations did call us the first begotten of the dead due to our false beliefs in Jesus and or Zeus.

We've become followers instead of leaders.

We've become the sellouts. No, we were the original sell outs that sold out Lovey not Jesus, but Lovey for dirty pieces of silver, and den tun roune sey wi nuh dweet when we did.

We are not loyal, so why the hell should Lovey remember us and be loyal to us? He's been trying with us and instead of listening; we continue to cry wolf an cry fi mercy. WELL NO MORE MERCY IS GIVEN BECAUSE LOVEY HAS STOPPED LISTENING. ZION FELL THIS YEAR AND THE ASIANS ARE POISED TO TAKE CONTROL AND RIGHTFULLY SO.

<u>Lovey is not politics nor is Lovey religion. Both are a condemnation of self thus the blood that is spilt by both.</u>

So truly good luck to some of you because all that is to come NOTHING CAN STOP IT NOW. THE SINKING OF LANDS HAVE AND HAS BEEN ORDAINED. THE DEATH OF MAN; BILLIONS HAVE BEEN COMMISSIONED AND OR ORDAINED. SO WHAT ARE YOU GOING TO DO BETWEEN NOW AND 2032?

In all we did, we did not see the bigger picture, that which is life itself. We did not see the truth; therefore, we could not see everlasting life. All we saw was death. Wicked and evil men did give you death hence the commissioning of man's evil book; your so called holy bible that billions globally believe in. And like I said, what you believe in is what's taking you to hell to die' burn. You wanted death and death is given. *No one can blame Lovey for this; hence WILL WAS THE FIRST CREATION. THE CHOICE TO CHOOSE BETWEEN GOOD AND EVIL, AND WE AS HUMANS DID CHOOSE THE LATTER; EVIL.*

But this is not true or right you are saying. It's farfetched you are blurting out and want to cuss me out and throw this book at the wall and me. Burn this book if you want I truly do not care nor do I give a damn. **_You got the message and you refused it._**

Listen, I know death and death know me.

I know life and life know me.

Either way, I know good and evil; life and death. It prophets me, woops profits me nothing to lie and deceive you. Life, good and true life is my choice, thus I cannot lie to you. If you find I am lying then truly forgive me as it is not intentional and yes damn well point out my lies. If you don't I will hold you accountable.

No you can't you're are saying.

Yes I can and will because I told you, if I am lying to forgive me and point out my lies. I do not set out to lie and deceive anyone. I write and write and the undertone sometimes are truly not right and I tell you of this. This is me, therefore I tell you to truly get to know me. I am harsh in words and I have to be because many of us are not learning. Lovey do not stop you from having your millions and billions even trillions, but make sure your business and personal dealings are clean; honest.

So, if you are a cheater and have women and men here, there and everywhere, slowly stop this nastiness. Do not think of the money and or luxuries you will lose. Think of the life you will gain in the end.

Yes this is your decision and right and I have no right to tell you what to do. You have Will and you made that choice; so truly forgive me. Like I said, life is worth it and the life you save might just be your own.

If you are good and true, do not write laws to accommodate death because death takes away from all. In the end you are the one to regret it. If you are clean continue to be clean. And if you so decide to come on board by walking clean; don't think your life is going to be easy because it truly won't be. You will be tested and tried like Job in your so called Holy Book. He was tested but his truth and true love saved him. I go through hell and you see this in some of these books. I see things before they happen thus I do go ballistic. LIFE IS GIVEN; WHY CHOOSE DEATH? Come on now.

Truth do not lie, hence I truly do not have the scrolls of man to teach you nor do I want or need them in truth. What is shown to me is what I give back to you. Like you I am learning and it's not easy. ***It will be hard in the beginning because we are conditioned by the clergy; demented sociopaths that write books of lies and give to you saying it's the truth.*** And yes you can say I am a part of the demented sociopaths because I am writing books. Thus judge not lest though be judged.

Smile.

Off course with my thoughts but hey, this is me.

There is a question that you are asking but I truly do not know how to ask it for you. So I am going to give you the answer.

BECAUSE WE ARE PHYSICAL BEINGS AND NOT TRULY SPIRITUAL BEINGS, LOVEY SHOWS US THINGS IN THE PHYSICAL AND OR IN HUMAN FORM. IF WE WERE TRULY SPIRITUAL AND NOT BOTH; WE WOULD SEE THINGS IN THE SPIRITUAL REALM INCLUDING LOVEY AND ALL THAT SURROUNDS HIM. MEANING THERE WOULD BE NO REASON TO SHOW US THINGS LIKE OUR END HERE ON EARTH.

IF WE WERE TRULY TRUE AND TRULY SPIRITUAL, WE WOULD NOT BE STUCK HERE ON EARTH. WE WOULD BE WITH LOVEY IN HIS ABODE.

IT IS BECAUSE OF SIN AND OR DISOBEDIENCE THAT LOVEY LEAVE US. WE ARE NOT CLEAN ENOUGH. And I hope I've answered your question to your suitability.

On earth and or here on earth, we are fleshy so we see things in the flesh; fleshy form and not spiritual form.

But when we die? You are still in fleshy form because you carry your fleshy signature and or hue with you to the grave. True spirits you cannot see because they have no hue and or fleshy hue. Our eyes are not clean and pure enough for us to see them.

Yes they can talk to you but you cannot see them.

Have I been dreaming some weird things lately?

Yes.

Dreamt a cactus tree or plant, prickly cactus was by my side. I looked up the meaning and was disgruntled by the meaning, thus I am so going to leave this alone. Not everything on the internet is true and it's not many that can truly interpret dreams.

Dreamt my feet and or I was standing in water, clear water on my balcony. The water was a quarter of the balcony. And no my balcony cannot hold water.

Dreamt I saw superman in the sky. Yes this was after my tirade with Lovey. So after some consideration I talked to Lovey. I think I said, really. People, you know Superman has a weakness right. You know Kryptonite makes Superman weak right. ***Fam and people, I don't know why Lovey showed me Superman because all he's telling me is that he's weak and he can be defeated.*** If he was a true superman, all of earth would be rid of all sin and evil. He would get rid of it like Superman; by speeding around the planet earth and scooping up all the evil and wicked people of this earth and lock them away more than infinitely and indefinitely; more than forevermore in a place; hell, where there is no escape because they would die upon completion of their sentence. I truly don't know because Superman is truly not Lovey and never will be. Superman is not all powerful because Superman is flawed; has a weakness. Therefore, my dream world is truly getting whacked.

This morning October 24, 2015, dreamt about the WWE and that Hulk Hogan and some other wrestlers were fighting with them over money. The wage they were making was not suitable. I am so not going to put anything in this dream because usually when I dream about the WWE someone is going to die. So all I can do is watch and see who's going to die if anyone dies at all.

I dreamt other things that involved dogs and poop. Got to watch and see because crap is coming my way. I am so not into it with my family and their bullshit. Thus I saw a caged grey dog with a little bit of white on its face in a cage in my home. My last child brought two dogs home and I was livid. So, I so have to watch this dream because lately I am seeing problems, obeah, children and I am so not into it. The now generation has a mind of their own and they don't like to take good advice from grownups.

Their attitude is, don't tell me what to do, I know what I am doing.

I told my son, last child learn from my mistakes in life and he said, he cannot learn from my mistakes he has to learn from his own mistakes. That's true, but he can also learn from my mistakes and not make the same ones I did. I told him this but he said, he might make the same mistakes I did. Thus I cannot overstand his logic. If I you know that lying kills and you see the way lying is killing, why lie or walk in the realm of liars?

If I punch you and you see me getting arrested, dragged through the ringer; why go out there and punch someone? Learn that it is wrong and don't do the same thing. And no, I am not contradicting myself from what I've written a few pages above.

If I am in a relationship with you and you constantly hurt me; I leave, then come back and give you more chances and still you do not amend your dirty ways: I'm gone indefinitely. Learn from this and don't get into a relationship with an abusive and ambitionless person.

People like these are not for you because they cannot learn and will never learn due to their actions. Strive to make you happy and seek the help of Lovey in choosing a good and clean partner. He will show you the way.

I am not in a relationship. It's not that I don't want to be in one but each person I meet is flawed. Meaning; Lovey show me the person and their faults; thus that person I have to avoid and not get involved with. This has nothing to do with politics or religion; it has to do with cleanliness.

IF YOU ARE NOT CLEAN AND OR WALKING ON THE WAY OF CLEANLINESS; THEN CONSIDER YOURSELF CUT OFF FROM LOVEY. LOVEY WANTS NOTHING TO DO WITH YOU BECAUSE YOU ARE NOT TRUE, NOR ARE YOU TRUTHFUL. YOU WALK ON THE PATHWAY AND IN THE WAY OF DEATH. THEREFORE, YOU WILL NOT HAVE EVERLASTING LIFE. Remember, <u>the wages of sin is death, BUT TRUTH IS EVERLASTING LIFE.</u>

<u>So, if you are with Lovey and Lovey is with you, he does show you your enemies and he does let you know about the person you have chosen.</u>

Have I failed in the area of listening?

Yes. Thus I am telling you to listen to Lovey because he knows best when it comes to you and your future. A person that is truthful cannot walk on the path of evil.

● ● ●

A person that is truthful cannot lie to you.

If he or she does not know, they will tell you they truly do not know.

Are there many truthful people left globally?

From what I see and know, no. Listen, it's customary to lie because this is what we are given by Men. Our lives are based on lies of men.

Religion is based on lies of men and women including children.

Politics is based on lies of men and women.

Like I've said time and time again, we allow others to lie to us and we believe in these lies. Thus we are the ones to give rise to death. WE LET LIARS TELL US THAT IN ORDER TO SEE GOD, WE MUST DIE. WE DO NOT ASK THE QUESTION, WHICH GOD DO WE DIE TO SEE?

<u>NO ONE CAN DIE TO SEE LIFE. YOU HAVE TO LIVE LIFE. YOU DIE TO SEE DEATH AND THE DEMONS OF HELL. IF TRUTH IS EVERLASTING LIFE, WHY DO YOU HAVE TO DIE FOR THE TRUTH?</u>

• • •

WHY DO YOU HAVE TO DIE TO SEE THE TRUTH?

LOVEY ISN'T DEAD. LOVEY IS TRUE LIFE. SO WHY WANT TO DIE TO BE PUNISHED SEVERELY IN HELL WITH DEATH?

Why give up your life to death?

This makes no sense at all. You are not dead you are alive.

DO YOU NOT SEE LIFE IN THE LIVING?

CAN YOU SEE LIFE IN DEATH?

No one can see life in death. Once you are dead you are truly dead. Look at a dead body. Do you see life in that dead body?

So why do you think there is life in death when there isn't.

The greed of man is the greed of man. It's unfortunate that we as humans believe that THERE IS LIFE IN DEATH.

Thus because you believe in death, and do all for death; you must die and I've told you this.

Do not war with someone that do not know your truth and the true and living God.

Well he or she is a Satan worshipper.

So the hell what!!! That is his or her decision; choice. What right do you have to tell that person he or she is wrong?

That is blasphemy and you are going to hell you are saying. Now I ask you, show me hell because I know what hell looks like. I have seen hell.

Well I am a Christian and or a Muslim and you are going to hell and die for your words. ***HELLO, YOU ARE ALREADY THERE THUS YOU HAVE THESE BOOKS. YOU BELIEVE IN DEATH AND WORSHIP DEATH BECAUSE I TOLD YOU JESUS DOES NOT EXIST. YOU KEEP DEATH ALIVE WITH YOUR NASTINESS AND LIES ABOUT GOD AND OR LOVEY.***

You speak out of turn and tell lies on Lovey because ABSOLUTELY NOT ONE CAN SPEAK FOR LOVEY. LOVEY HAS A VOICE AND HE CAN SPEAK FOR HIMSELF AND HERSELF.

You as Christians, Catholics, Prostestants, Zionist, Anglicans, Adventists, Mormons, Muslims, Satanists, Latter Day Saints, Jehovah's Witnesses which is the devil's witnesses in blood sacrifices and all the nastiness of life and what have you and whatever else frauds that you call yourselves cannot speak for Lovey. Not one of you has a place with him. You believe in death and do all for death.

You worship and praise a **_MAN_** that you say was his son.

Now let me ask you this, **_WHAT MAN OR CHILD DID LOVEY GIVE TO YOU AND SAY; THIS IS MY SON YOU MUST WORSHIP HIM?_**

What man or child did Lovey tell you personally that he was going to give you and humanity as a sacrifice unto death?

Man Lovey must have hated his own child that he Lovey would sacrifice him unto death for death's wicked and evil own.

YOU IN THE RELIGIOUS WORLD SELL LIES AND TELL LIES ON LOVEY. HOW THE HELL CAN YOU DO THIS TO YOUR BELOVED?

How can you turn against Lovey like this?

You say you are of Lovey but in truth; you are of death because you praise and worship death; pay death for the lies that have been fed to you by your wicked and evil own. You want a saving grace, but how can Lovey save you if he Lovey knows you not? Wickedness is not a part of Lovey's realm and world. *Will was the first man, thus WILL IS TRULY UGLY. IT IS OUR WILL THAT LET US DO ALL THE UGLY AND UNCLEAN THINGS IN LIFE.*

If we as humans were clean, I would not have seen the Will; ugly will of man come on now. We say we love, but in truth, we do not love; we hate.

We spread hate and lie to one another. So, when we do all these evil things; *HOW CAN LOVEY LOOK TO US AND SAY YOU ARE MY CHILD AND WELL DONE?*

As humans we tell lies on him. Do all manner of evil against him and to him and he's to say, "oh, it's okay, I forgive you and will save you." Lovey cannot do this. I told you, I have to stop arguing with him for my children and some of you. I am sinning myself and disrespecting him and I cannot do this anymore. Yes I made him my ALL but it does not mean I should battle him for children and people that are truly not deserving of him. So in this sense I am the weak one. I am not strong, thus I saw Superman in the sky. I saw my weakness. I have to be strong now because like I said, the WILL OF MAN is truly ugly; hence I did not like Will.

TRUE LIFE CANNOT DIE THUS TRUTH IS EVERLASTING LIFE AND YOU HAVE TO LIVE YOUR LIFE GOOD AND TRUE.

Michelle Jean

Yes the dream world is getting weird again. It's October 25, 2015 and I kept dreaming about pools; pools with round steps leading into calm blue water.

Some of the pools had no steps and one pool was a gateway to the sea. The water was a little bit rough but you could walk in it. This family of 3 or four went swimming and they wanted me to come swim in the water. You could see their legs flapping away and they were having fun. One of children, a little girl said, Michelle come swim, but I could not swim and said to myself in the dream; I have to take swimming lessons.

Also dreamt Barak Obama. This was my final dream because my puppy rudely woke me up out of the dream with her loud barking. He was talking to this Indian journalist about erectile dysfunction in the dream. In the dream he had erectile dysfunction that had to do with his testicles or testies. In the dream he was given something ***called buruka and or burooka by his doctor.*** I believe the journalist asked him about it and he told him to ask his doctor, his doctor should know. In the dream he Barak did not give any information on the drug, but this drug worked for him in the dream. But before I saw him talking to the journalist it was if I was watching a video on drowning and I was a participant in the video. Someone drowned a woman that looked like Barbara Bush. People I truly do not know what a drowned dead body looks like in their decomposing state but this one was gross looking. I started to give the body which had a navel ring CPR not mouth to mouth. I was using my hand to compress the rib cage so that fluids would come out of the body. The weird part of the dream was, while giving CPR, it was as if I was seeing Barak's face now and not Barbara Bush's.

Truly weird.

And please truly do not quote me on the spelling of buruka or burooka. **BU** is the first two letters of the medication; this I know for sure. Like I said, my puppy started barking and I had to wake up out of my sleep.

Yea I am so finished editing this book and I am so not going over it again. This book is quite long. Oh man, I am so not finished because I did not include my writings from October 17, 2015.

Well here we go.

Michelle

<u>WRITINGS FROM OCTOBER 17, 2015</u>

It's time for me to bid you farewell Lovey.
It's time for me to let you go.
Time for me to be on my own without you.

Life is truly too hard with you and in truth, I cannot take the hardships with you.

It's like life means nothing to you.

You make no sense to me anymore; hence I can no longer hold on to you.

I can no longer have a one sided relationship with you.

Lovey, so many things affect me now. I cannot stand to see homelessness. It hurts me and bring me to tears to see people lying on sidewalks.

It hurts me to see people hungry, but yet politicians spend billions; trillions of dollars combined on war machines, war, diseases that kill. So Lovey you make no sense to me anymore. All these things are happening here on earth and you see but yet refuse to stop it. Earth has become the hot bed and dung of death and you truly don't care. So I have to leave you. I should not have to cry for the homeless in the street come on now man. Where is your compassion for the weak and have not?

I don't know. Maybe it's me.

Maybe I want to do so much and because I can't, I am taking it out on you. You know my soft spot for the homeless and needy Lovey; you truly know it.

Michelle

So I have to truly walk away from you Lovey because the ratio of evil to good is truly not fair.

Evil take away from the natural balance of all and you know this, but yet you leave everything in disarray; unbalanced.

I cannot live like this, thus I give you back all you've given me in truth and move forward with my best interest and my good and true life in hand.

I cannot live like the dead.

I cannot live caged, nor can I live in a noisy environment.

I have to truly find peace and I cannot find true peace in you or with you.

Nor can I find true peace here on earth and in the universe. So because of this and more, I have to once again truly divorce you.

I am seeking truth in you but in all I find, I find I have to beg you like a beggar; a homeless person.

Why should I have to beg you for anything Lovey?

Does truth not provide truthfully?

Can anyone live peacefully in an unbalanced world and society?

So why are you unfair to your own chosen people?

Why be like the politicians of this world?

Once they are elected into office they forget the people that voted them in and treat them like dirt.

Do you not do the same thing to those who have and has chosen you Lovey?

Do you not ignore us and side with death and their people against us?

Thus death's people can reach us, obeah us and kill us.

Michelle

So as you have left me, I have to leave you also.

No, I will not turn against you, but the relationship we have must be terminated and I have to go on living my life without you.

My journey with you have and has come to an end with me. I truly hope the next person you choose and chose to write; you are truthful and kind, truly helpful and truly giving to them.

I truly hope you do not leave them in financial ruin as you did me.

I truly hope you do not leave them in emotional ruin as you've done me.

I truly hope you care for them and lead them right; truly be there for them physically and emotionally.

I truly, truly, truly hope you do not abandon them and leave them broken as you've done me.

Truly keep that person Lovey and truly help them financially, health wise, emotionally, spiritually, and physically amongst other things.

For me, please treat the next person good and never let them feel as if you are not there for them. Never let evil come near them or come in their home as you've done me.

Keep them save and protected at all time. Know that I am sorry it did not work out for us and you will remain in my heart for all lifetime.

Truly be good to you and take care of yourself.

True love always.

Michelle

So as I go my way and leave you Lovey, I wish you all the best in life.

I wish you true joy and happiness, true peace and true love always.

As a daughter, I wish you could have truly been there for me financially, emotionally and health wise.

In all I do, I truly hope you learnt something good and positive, true and clean from me.

Every child need a father Lovey and it's disheartening to know that as a father, you are truly not there for us to guide us truthfully.

It's disheartening to know that you put evil above good.

Disheartening to know that when we cry out to you for help, you are truly not there.

No one should have to leave you Lovey but as I grew and learn, I found out, no one truly stays with you because we feel caged; limited in what we can do.

We are left lonely; at least I am.

We are left abandoned; without a true partner; well at least I am.

I am left feeling broken; abused by you.

Thus anyone that lives in an abusive relationship seek ways to get out of them.

I am seeking ways to leave our abusive relationship Lovey.

Thus I am out, no longer walking with you for my own good in goodness and in truth.

You are abusive Lovey and you cannot say otherwise because my mental and or spiritual scars are there as proof.

Michelle

There is nothing beautiful about depression Lovey.

Nothing beautiful in physical and spiritual abuse.

There is nothing beautiful in having a spiritual father that neglects you; truly can't help you.

Time and time again you've shown me on my own; left to find my own way and there is truly nothing beautiful in being abandoned.

Yes tears come and go, but what is the point in having a father than cannot help you?

What is the point of having a father that cannot truly protect you from all facets of wickedness and evil?

Evil reach me, thus evil is more powerful than you Lovey.

So how can you be a true builder; creator, if evil can tumble down and destroy all including your good and true people so easily?

You did abandon us; therefore we are lost. We can't find you and never will be able to find you given the state we are in.

So no Lovey, I cannot continue to sojourn with you because in truth and to me, there is no fairness in you.

You cannot say you love so and watch wicked and evil men and women including children take the lives and freedom of your good and true people.

When you do this, you do not love them or truly love them; you hate them.

You can no longer stand on the sidelines of death and watch those devoted and truly love you be killed by the wicked and evil come on now.

Michelle

Those are just a little something I wrote to Lovey on October 17, 2015. It is disheartening to know that our lives here on earth is messed up in some way. We all have issues and these issues (my issues) I take to Lovey in anger and in truth. Yes we truly need him but Lovey truly need to communicate better with his good and true people. I know the earth is filled with sin and there is so much Lovey can do. Yes the time of harvesting is almost upon us, but if he had truly needed me to prepare a place for him and you; he would truly help me to do so and stop dilly dallying by hindering me come on now. Yes I have to give him time but there is so much time I can give. I am up there in age and I too need to live my life in a clean, true, positive and good way, and I cannot do this living amongst the evil and unclean.

Michelle

SONG SELECTIONS

BAM BAM   Sister Nancy

Wow this song brings back memories. Thus Kat DaLuna and Trey Songz sampled this song (Bam Bam) with BUM BUM. Kat if yu a chat bout bum bum yu fi ha batty fi show or don't show yu batty (bum bum) at all. Did not like the video as it was truly tasteless and tacky. You are talented and you truly do not have to sell yourself short like this to prove a point. Please revamp yourself and stop with the nudity. Like I said, you are talented.

Patra, Lady P, yu an Lady Saw a share notes and or lyrics. She too don't like fi wine inna public, she wine inna bed. Wow and that's all I got to say.

People do check out Razz Attack Riddim Medley, the full version. This medley wicked (hot) mi a tell yu.   Please don't watch the language.

DIS A DI BESS   Dexta Daps

But Dexta di cush soh bad dat dem haffi sen plane fi fine yu cause yu soh high. Blurnaught Jamaican Cush a di bess, betta dan di hard drugs dem a sell fi real.

WE REACH   Dexta Daps
WE A RAVE   Dexta Daps

CHEAT ON YOU   Dexta Daps

I so need the clean version of this song.

REAL FREN   Dexta Daps

TONIGHT   *Dexta Daps*
I so need the clean version of this song.

WINE FOR ME   *Dexta Daps*

There are more songs I wrote down on another paper but I can't find it. If I have another book and I find the list; I will make sure I include them.

Do take care and truly live clean. Listen, I can only push the songs I find with a meaning and or I truly like. I do not know these artists nor do I know the their content of character apart for what's shown to me in my visions. I do not see all thus what I see I tell you about them. As for the artists themselves I endorse none on a personal or professional level. I can only tell you about these songs and their meanings on a different level.

Oh before I go, check out DJ Marcus's 90s Dancehall Style.

Michelle

OTHER BOOKS BY MICHELLE JEAN

Blackman Redemption – The Fall of Michelle Jean
Blackman Redemption – After the Fall Apology
Blackman Redemption – World Cry – Christine Lewis
Blackman Redemption
Blackman Redemption – The Rise and Fall of Jamaica
Blackman Redemption – The War of Israel
Blackman Redemption – The Way I Speak to God
Blackman Redemption – A Little Talk With Man
Blackman Redemption – The Den of Thieves
Blackman Redemption – The Death of Jamaica
Blackman Redemption – Happy Mother's Day
Blackman Redemption – The Death of Faith
Blackman Redemption – The War of Religion
Blackman Redemption – The Death of Russia
Blackman Redemption – The Truth
Blackman Redemption – Spiritual War
Blackman Redemption – The Youths
Blackman Redemption – Black Man Where Is Your God?

The New Book of Life
The New Book of Life – A Cry For The Children
The New Book of Life – Judgement
The New Book of Life – Love Bound
The New Book of Life – Me
The New Book of Life – Life

Just One of Those Days
Book Two – Just One of Those Days
Just One of Those Days – Book Three The Way I Feel
Just One of Those Days – Book Four

The Days I Am Weak
Crazy Thoughts – My Book of Sin
Broken
Ode to Mr. Dean Fraser

A Little Little Talk
A Little Little Talk – Book Two

Prayers
My Collective
A Little Talk/ A Time For Fun and Play
Simple Poems
Behind The Scars
Songs of Praise And Love

Love Bound
Love Bound – Book Two

Dedication Unto My Kids
More Talk
Saving America From A Woman's Perspective
My Collective the Other Side of Me
My Collective the Dark Side of Me
A Blessed Day
Lose To Win
My Doubtful Days – Book One

My Little Talk With God
My Little Talk With God – Book Two

A Different Mood and World – Thinking

My Nagging Day
My Nagging Day – Book Two
Friday September 13, 2013
My True Love
It Would Be You
My Day

A Little Advice – Talk
1313, 2032, 2132 – The End of Man
Tata

MICHELLE'S BOOK BLOG – BOOKS 1 – 22

My Problem Day
A Better Way
Stay – Adultery and the Weight of Sin – Cleanliness Message

Let's Talk
Lonely Days – Foundation
A Little Talk With Jamaica – As Long As I Live
Instructions For Death
My Lonely Thoughts
My Lonely Thoughts – Book Two
My Morning Talks – Prayers With God
What A Mess
My Little Book
A Little Word With You
My First Trip of 2015
Black Mother – Mama Africa
Islamic Thought
My California Trip January 2015
My True Devotion by Michelle – Michelle Jean
My Many Questions To God
My Talk
My Talk Book Two
My Talk Book Three – The Rise of Michelle Jean
My Talk Book Four
My Talk Book Five
My Talk Book Six
My Talk Book Seven
My Talk Book Eight – My Depression
My Talk Book Nine – Death
My Talk Book Ten – Wow
My Day – Book Two
My Talk Book Eleven – What About December?
Haven Hill
What About December – Book Two
My Talk Book Twelve – Summary and or Confusion
My Talk Book Thirteen
My Talk Book Fourteen – My Talk With God
My Talk Book Fifteen – My Talk
My Thoughts – Freedom